THE TEETH OF TIME

Footprints Series
JANE ERRINGTON, Editor

The life stories of individual women and men who were participants
in interesting events help nuance larger historical narratives, at times
reinforcing those narratives, at other times contradicting them. The
Footprints series introduces extraordinary Canadians, past and present,
who have led fascinating and important lives at home and throughout
the world.

The series includes primarily original manuscripts but may consider
the English-language translation of works that have already appeared
in another language. The editor of the series welcomes inquiries from
authors. If you are in the process of completing a manuscript that
you think might fit into the series, please contact her, care of McGill-
Queen's University Press, 3430 McTavish Street, Montreal, QC H3A 1X9.

Blatant Injustice
*The Story of a Jewish Refugee from Nazi Germany Imprisoned
in Britain and Canada during World War II*
Walter W. Igersheimer
Edited and with a foreword by Ian Darragh

Against the Current
Memoirs
Boris Ragula

Margaret Macdonald
Imperial Daughter
Susan Mann

My Life at the Bar and Beyond
Alex K. Paterson

Red Travellers
Jeanne Corbin and Her Comrades
Andrée Lévesque

The Teeth of Time
Remembering Pierre Elliott Trudeau
Ramsay Cook

THE TEETH OF TIME

REMEMBERING PIERRE ELLIOTT TRUDEAU

RAMSAY COOK

McGILL-QUEEN'S UNIVERSITY PRESS

Montreal & Kingston · London · Ithaca

ISBN-13: 978-0-7735-3149-9
ISBN-10: 0-7735-3149-1

Legal deposit third quarter 2006
Bibliothèque nationale du Québec

Printed in Canada on acid-free paper.

McGill-Queen's University Press acknowledges the support of the Canada
Council for the Arts for our publishing program. We also acknowledge
the financial support of the Government of Canada through the Book
Publishing Industry Development Program (BPIDP) for our publishing
activities.

Illustrations pages 125 and 184 published courtesy Jean-Marc Carisse;
page 180 courtesy Desmond Glynn; page 53 courtesy York University,
Clara Thomas Archives, ASC1075

Library and Archives Canada Cataloguing in Publication

Cook, Ramsay, 1931–
The teeth of time : remembering Pierre Elliott Trudeau / Ramsay Cook.

(Footprint series)
Includes bibliographical references and index.

ISBN-13: 978-0-7735-3149-9
ISBN-10: 0-7735-3149-1

1. Trudeau, Pierre Elliott, 1919–2000. 2. Prime ministers – Canada –
Biography. 3. Trudeau, Pierre Elliott, 1919–2000 – Friends and associates.
4. Cook, Ramsay, 1931–.
I. Title. II. Series.

FC626.T7C65 2006   971.064'4092   C2006-902353-0

This book was designed and typeset by
studio oneonone in Sabon 10.3/14

To
Jacqueline and Blair Neatby
&
Jack Saywell

for years of generous friendship

CONTENTS

Preface / ix

Acknowledgments / xi

Prologue: Sir Wilfrid Laurier, O.D. Skelton,
J.W. Dafoe, Pierre Elliott Trudeau, and Me / 3

ONE Intellectual Friends / 8

TWO Liberal Malgré Lui / 40

THREE A Friend in Power / 79

FOUR Liberty Infringed / 103

FIVE Rights and Freedoms Entrenched / 123

SIX Friends / 148

APPENDICES

1 What's Special about the NDP's Status for Quebec? / 187

2 History Will Measure Trudeau against Laurier / 197

Notes / 205

Index / 211

PREFACE

It is difficult for a man to speak long of himself without Vanity:
Therefore I shall be short.

DAVID HUME *My Own Life*, 1776

Pierre Trudeau's death on 28 September 2000 affected me very
deeply. We had known each other for nearly forty years. During the following weeks I spent many hours recalling those years
and thinking about Pierre Trudeau. A few months later, having read and heard so many comments on Trudeau's life and
work, I decided to write a brief account of our friendship. At
first it was an exercise in self-understanding, a catharsis, aimed
at getting my mind off those memories. Occasionally I checked
my files to confirm a date, to remind myself of conversations,
or to recover the feeling of times past. Gradually the personal
memoir and the historical record became intertwined in a manner that interested me as an historian. So I began to look more
systematically at my documents and to think more about the
form that was beginning to emerge – a reconstructed diary, a
memoir with documents, an autobiography, or maybe just an
exercise in vanity? All of the above, not a history of the Trudeau
years but my "remembrance of things past" – *à la recherche
du temps perdu* – my attempt to "break the teeth of Time."

Once a draft had been completed, I set it aside, the catharsis
mostly accomplished. Several years passed before I returned
to it. Then, after some revision and much hesitation, I decided to publish this account of a somewhat unusual friendship.
But why? I could, I suppose, attempt to disguise this display

of self-importance by a well-established memorialist's strategy: I wrote it for my family. But a few xeroxed copies would satisfy that demand. Anyway, Eleanor, Maggi, and Mark have all heard most of this before and sometimes were part of the past that I have remembered. Perhaps I could claim to have recorded these memories for the members of Trudeau's family. That would only slightly increase the xeroxing. Anyway, they already know what is most important about their father and need no help from me. So all that I can say in self-defence is that this memoir remains, at least in large part, an attempt to understand my friendship with a remarkable person. But I hope that my notes and observations contain some scraps of information that may be useful to future biographers and historians who are seeking to understand Pierre Trudeau and his times. This memoir, then, is for me and for them and, I hope, for curious readers who did not share my good fortune in having a forty-year discussion with Pierre Elliott Trudeau – a lucid, courageous, generous, quick-witted friend who, to my astonishment, became the prime minister of our country. The book is short and I hope therefore not too vain.

RAMSAY COOK
Tenpenny Lake, Quebec
23 August 2005

ACKNOWLEDGMENTS

Even memories require the help of others, at least if you hope to get them right. Eleanor, Maggi, and Mark read and commented on my manuscript, jogged and corrected my memories about the past that we all shared. Eleanor, in addition to helping me shape the story, gave me the use of an account she kept of one of the essential events described in this book. These memories are then, in a real sense, the Cooks' memories. Of course, I am indebted to my family for much more: for love, support, talk, and laughter. Vera, Katherine, and Joshua deserve affectionate thanks, too.

Marc Lalonde and Alexandre Trudeau, on behalf of the Trudeau literary executors, kindly granted me permission to quote from the letters written to me by my friend. M. Lalonde also agreed to my use of his letters. John English, whose full-scale life of Pierre Trudeau will reveal much more of the man's career than I have attempted, generously facilitated this permission and often talked with me about our common interest.

Credits for the photographs belong to Jean-Marc Carisse, the Clara Thomas Archives at York University, and Desmond Glynn.

The anonymous readers of my manuscript made helpful suggestions that I have carefully considered and often accepted. I thank them for their criticisms and for their support. I gratefully acknowledge the skilful, careful editorial work done by

Carlotta Lemieux, who prepared my manuscript for publication. Philip Cercone, Joan McGilvray, and the staff at McGill-Queen's University Press worked overtime to meet a very tight schedule. All of these people make it easy for me to acknowledge that I alone am responsible for any deficiencies that remain.

I have dedicated this memoir to three wonderful friends who, for good reason, sometimes appear in it. They are certainly a vivid part of my memories of good times past.

RAMSAY COOK

THE TEETH OF TIME

We differ from other states in regarding the man who holds aloof from public life not as "quiet" but as useless; we decide or debate, carefully and in person, all matters of policy, holding, not that words and deeds go ill together, but that acts are foredoomed to failure when undertaken undiscussed. For we are noted for being at once most adventurous in action and most reflective beforehand ... But the bravest are surely those who have the clearest vision of what is before them, glory and danger alike, and yet notwithstanding go out to meet it.

THUCYDIDES, *The History of the Peloponnesian War*

Sir Wilfrid Laurier, O.D. Skelton, J.W. Dafoe, Pierre Elliott Trudeau, and Me

History is a very curious thing ... It exists only in the memories of people.

PIERRE ELLIOTT TRUDEAU, 1993

Pierre Trudeau and I sometimes talked about Canadian history but never about his prospective place in it. He preferred to analyse his own times and speculate about the future, believing that societies and individuals that dwell on their past – even yearn for a future that will recreate the past – would become anachronisms. Quebec before 1960, the Quebec that formed him, demonstrated this truth. The message of the most important text Trudeau ever wrote, his powerful opening essay in *La grève de l'amiante,* was that Quebec's intellectual and social conservatism derived from imagining a glorious past, decrying a misunderstood present, and dreaming of a utopian future. Sometimes he seemed to suggest that history was little more than a burden to be thrown off. Nevertheless, he knew and loved classical history, and as his essays revealed, he had read widely in the history of the contemporary world, including Canada. And it is clear from his decision to participate in the production of a television series on his life and career, and from the publication of his *Memoirs,* that he was interested in his place in history – though not concerned enough to write a thorough account of it.

He cooperated, within limits, with successive biographers who chronicled his career while he was still alive: Richard Gwyn, George Radwanski, Christina McCall, and Stephen Clarkson. I doubt that he ever read these books. His conversations, at least with me, were rarely about his past. Reminiscence was not his style. Still, I was often struck by his memories of friends – where and when he had first met them or last seen them. At our house in November 1970, not having seen my wife Eleanor since 1961, he immediately recalled my telling him that she had been expecting a child in 1963 when he and I had acted as chaperones for a student conference in Toronto. If he kept a regular diary – and I doubt that he did – he never mentioned it.

Did he care about his reputation and how he would be remembered? Obviously he did. But like those writers who want only their published work to be judged by the future, leaving their lives anonymous, Trudeau remained a private man whose public life was found in his writings and in his political action. About the rest he was guarded, even shy, willing to slip quietly out of the public view on his retirement, at least until the principles of the 1982 constitution were threatened. Though I thought he once or twice hinted that I might write his biography, my suggestion that I do a partial study of his constitutional thought and action evoked no real interest. He seemed satisfied that the future would take care of itself, provided that his writings were available to readers. Most of them are, in new editions, though *La grève de l'amiante*, alas, is out of print. He preferred that his own words be read rather than filtered through another set of eyes – even, perhaps, friendly eyes. As a politician he often chose to speak directly to his constituency rather than through an interviewer. As I have reason to know, he preferred his own speeches to those written for him. He was always at his oratorical best speaking his own words.

When he thought about the past, the Canadian political past, his mind turned to Sir Wilfrid Laurier. This was natural enough. Both were bilingual French Canadian intellectuals whose political careers focused on national unity themes. Both were distrusted and vilified by the nationalist leaders of their home province. Trudeau's response to Quebec nationalists' claims that the federal government ignored French Canadian interests was to call up Laurier (even exaggerating for polemical purposes) as the single example of a French Canadian who had made any real impact in Ottawa. Unfair as this sweeping claim was to Ernest Lapointe, Louis St Laurent, and others, it revealed his model of what became known as "French power" when *les trois colombes* – Jean Marchand, Gérard Pelletier, and Trudeau – set out for Ottawa in 1965. Laurier was the prime minister about whom he questioned me when we talked one evening at the Royal York Hotel as he weighed the arguments for and against entering his party's leadership contest. He already knew that Laurier, the French Canadian, had made himself "indispensable to the history of Canada." But how had he stood the test of time in Quebec?

Naturally, then, I thought first of Laurier's biographer, the Queen's professor O.D. Skelton, when shortly after Trudeau's death his literary executors approached me with the suggestion that I write the "official" biography. Skelton had been close to Laurier in his later years and shared most of this first French Canadian prime minister's views, especially on the constitution and on Canada's place in the world. Both believed that Canada should press for independence – or, rather, for complete autonomy – while formally maintaining the British connection. Skelton's later career as a public servant was guided by the conviction that isolation from world affairs alone would save Canada from another tragedy of the sort suffered in 1917: deep division between French and English, the near destruction of Laurier's dream. Some time before his death in early 1919, Laurier turned most of his private papers over to Skelton, and Lady Laurier gave him the remainder after her husband died. Skelton's two-volume *Life and Letters of Sir Wilfrid Laurier*, long the standard work on Sir Wilfrid, advanced an interpretation which the Queen's University professor set out in his preface. His pages, he wrote in 1921, were "given to the public with the hope that they may provide his countrymen with the material for a fuller understanding of one who was not only a moving orator, a skilled parliamentarian, a courageous party leader, and a faithful servant of his country, but who was the finest and simplest gentleman, the noblest and most unselfish man, it has ever been my good fortune to know."[1]

Some variation on these sentiments, I thought, I could write about Pierre Trudeau as I had known him. But as a biographer of John Wesley Dafoe, I also remembered the four-part critique which that great editor had written of Skelton's book and later published as *Laurier: A Study in Canadian Politics*. "Men may fail to be heroes to their valets," Dafoe wrote, "but they are more successful with their biographers."[2] He went on to predict that a future biographer would likely find that Laurier "had affinities with Macchiavelli as well as with Sir Galahad." My own research suggested that Dafoe had been right not just about Laurier but about virtually all the successful politicians that I had studied and observed – and even some unsuccessful ones. The great English historian Lord Acton confirmed this conviction. As I read through hundreds of volumes of Laurier papers, I came across letters that Skelton had missed or chosen not to use, notably a few letters from the 1870s that were so critical of the Quebec church that they were still restricted in the 1950s, though no one seemed to know why any longer. Then there were the sources which Skelton had not been able to examine but which often cast Laurier in another light – Dafoe's light. The valet had never been consulted. Skelton was not dishonest, far from it. But his perspective as a friend and admirer coloured the glass through which he examined his subject.

In later years, I often thought about this experience and realized that writing the biography of a friend has many pitfalls, pitfalls that could best be avoided by not writing the biography. At least twice before I had stuck firmly to this conclusion. So while flattered to be nominated as biographer of this endlessly fascinating prime minister, I declined. That way my independence, something Trudeau had always valued, is preserved. I leave it for another biographer to discover what mixture of Machiavelli and Sir Galahad made him the brave leader that he undoubtedly was. In time, too, even the valet may reveal some of his secrets. Still, friends know things and have viewpoints that biographers, even "detached" biographers, might value. So, despite my undisguised bias, these glimpses of Pierre Trudeau may help in drawing up the final balance sheet. And for me, writing this memoir, like knowing Pierre Trudeau, has been an intellectual adventure in self-understanding.

ONE

INTELLECTUAL FRIENDS

> We differ from other states in regarding the man who holds aloof
> from public life not as "quiet" but as useless.
>
> THUCYDIDES, *The History of the Peloponnesian War*

FRIENDSHIP

Friendship has more than one meaning. In a close personal
friendship almost everything, even the most private, is shared.
Pierre Trudeau had such friends: Jacques Hébert, Jean March-
and, Marc Lalonde, certainly Gérard Pelletier, and perhaps others. They knew the private man, and they knew that intimate
friendship meant keeping it private. Then there are casual friends,
acquaintances. Everyone, and especially every public figure, has
many. I had a third kind of friendship with Trudeau: a forty-
year intellectual friendship, based on shared convictions that grew
out of remarkably different pasts. Twelve years my senior,
Trudeau was the son of a successful French Canadian business-
man, reportedly a notable man-about-town, who owned, among
other things, shares in the Montreal Royals baseball team. His
mother was a highly cultured woman of dual linguistic heritage. Both parents were faithful Catholics. I was the son of an
immigrant farm labourer from a once prosperous English family – who later became a small-town Protestant clergyman – and

a gentle farm-born mother of Methodist and Orange ancestry. They owned almost nothing. I played second base for the Morden Legionnaires. Both Trudeau and I enjoyed competitive athletics: he liked to compete against himself; I happily took on others. We both took to the water: he canoed, I swam. Apart from a wartime visit to Victoria, British Columbia, and a brief stint picking potatoes one autumn in Walhalla, North Dakota, I never left the Canadian prairies until I was twenty. By the time he reached that age, Trudeau had seen much of Europe, and after a private school education at Collège Jean-de-Brébeuf in Montreal, he had studied at the best universities in North America, France, and Great Britain. Following my graduation from Maple Leaf Collegiate Institute in Morden, Manitoba, I had headed to United College in Winnipeg and then to Queen's University and the University of Toronto. Almost by accident I became a professional historian. He chose the life of a freelance lawyer and intellectual. When we first met in 1961, he drove a Mercedes-Benz SL roadster; I had recently acquired a Morris Minor – "pre-owned."

Gradually, over nearly forty years, we found that we held many of the same basic ideas about major public questions, both Canadian and international. This I discovered initially through reading Trudeau and later by watching his actions both before and during his years in politics. He came to know me partly in the same way: I translated his articles for the *Canadian Forum*; he read what I wrote for *Le Devoir* and the *Montreal Star*; and he encouraged me to publish in *Cité libre*. Because of our commonly held convictions, we worked together on occasional projects, including the one that made him prime minister. Then he had the chance and the determination to implement these shared ideas, which brought me both closer to him intellectually and farther away personally. His death ended our friendship, as it ended the life of the most extraordinary man I have ever known.

DISCOVERY

Appropriately enough, I first met Trudeau on the printed page. During the spring of 1955 at Queen's University, where I was enrolled in the Master of Arts program, I participated in a seminar on French Canada directed by Arthur Lower and Fred Gibson. A classmate named John Lynch-Staunton (later deputy mayor of Montreal and then a Conservative senator) had returned from a weekend in Montreal to report, somewhat excitedly, that a new radical, anticlerical magazine had been founded in Quebec. In fact, *Cité libre* was already five years old. Even so, it had not yet appeared in the Queen's library. But under Lower's tutelage I had acquired the habit of reading *Le Devoir*. There I not only developed a fascination with the subtle nationalist mind of André Laurendeau, the paper's editor, but also occasionally discovered articles about *Cité libre* and sometimes articles by contributors to that somewhat irregular publication.

Reading *Le Devoir*, I learned of the publication in early 1956 of one of the most important books in the modern intellectual history of Quebec, *La grève de l'amiante*. In June I bought a copy in Ottawa, where I was doing research at the Public Archives (as they were then known). Trudeau's essay, "La province de Québec au moment de la grève" was a *tour de force*, particularly the long section under the subheading "Les idées." It documented the centrality of nationalism to French Canadian political and social thought, and then proceeded to demonstrate the irrelevance of these ideas to the so-

cial and economic realities of modern Quebec. It
ly with a quotation from Ecclesiastes, "*mataiotè
ta panta mataiotès,*" sending us non-classicists
dictionaries, if not to the Septuagint.[1] In *Le Devo*
tober 1956, in an editorial entitled "Sur cents pa⌣⌣ ae P.-E.
Trudeau," Laurendeau critically appraised this brilliant essay
and made it clear to me that in Pierre Trudeau I had met a mind
to which I was immediately attracted, a mind learned, incisive,
and engaged – a powerful reason and a deep passion.

ANTINATIONALIST UNITY

As an undergraduate I developed doubts about nationalism,
especially while studying it with Professor W.J. Rose, an expert on Poland and Eastern Europe, who taught at United College in 1953–54. In this course I learned of Tomas Masaryk, a
Czech philosopher and patriot who, in contrast to most of the
nationalists of his day, advocated a reformed multinational
Hapsburg Empire rather than national self-determination. The
fate of his small democracy after 1938 demonstrated his pre-
science. A year later, in Ottawa, I bought a book that confirmed my doubts. George Orwell's 1953 collection *England
Your England and Other Essays* included his brilliant "Notes
on Nationalism." Orwell, like Trudeau, rejected overarching
ideologies, observed the indifference of nationalists to reality,
and distinguished between patriotism and nationalism. He
wrote the following sentence, which has always stayed with
me: "Every nationalist is haunted by the belief that the past
can be altered."[2] This incisive insight neatly summarizes
Trudeau's indictment of French Canadian nationalism. Although Trudeau may not have known of Orwell's essay (and I
can't remember ever asking him), he certainly read another

English thinker whose work I, too, had come to admire in the mid-fifties: Lord Acton.

While supervising my master's thesis on civil liberties in Canada during the Second World War, Lower had insisted that I read widely on liberalism, civil liberties, bills of rights, and related subjects. A book that especially impressed me was Acton's *The History of Freedom and Other Essays*, which included his famous essay on nationality. This essay was also meat and drink for Trudeau, though I have no idea when he first came across it. In it he found, as I did, a vigorous critique of such liberals as John Stuart Mill, who viewed the nineteenth-century nationalist demand for the right of self-determination for all ethnically homogeneous groups as a natural and desirable extension of liberalism. Acton replied that national homogeneity threatened freedom rather than nurturing it; multinational states, where groups counterbalanced each other, were far more likely to respect and promote both individual freedom and cultural pluralism.

On first reading Acton, I thought of Canada, where cultural diversity was the ideal, not the reality. Nationalism, he argued, "does not aim at either liberty or prosperity, both of which it sacrifices to the imperative necessity of making the nation the mould and measure of the State.[3] In my first scholarly article, published in the *Canadian Historical Review* in 1958, I illustrated this argument. The article, which dealt with the struggle over minority school rights in Manitoba and the territory of Keewatin, concluded that "while national unity had been preserved a price had to be paid ... the long-suffering minority in Manitoba gained little."[4] Acton informed and was quoted in Trudeau's passionate 1962 denunciation of separatism entitled "La nouvelle trahison des clercs." It was the first Trudeau essay that I translated, with Eleanor's help, for publication in the *Canadian Forum*. I did so partly because it contained this essentially Actonian opening sentence: "It is not the concept of *nation* that is retrograde; it is the idea that the nation must necessarily be sovereign."[5] (Acton had described nationalism as "a retrograde step in history" because it demanded that the "State and the nation" coincide.)[6]

Trudeau had read widely on nationalism, in both French and English, long before we came to know each other and began to discuss the renewal of an ideology that seemed in decline after the Second World War. The only study of this subject that I drew to his attention was Elie Kedourie's *Nationalism* (1960), a profound philosophical analysis of the Herderian and Kantian intellectual precepts that underlay nineteenth-century nationalism. Trudeau found its intellectual rigour and its negative assessment of the ideology convincing. In the Quebec of the 1960s, Kedourie's emphasis on the role of youth in nationalist movements (he described nationalist movements as "children's crusades")[7] and the generational conflict it masked seemed especially apposite. In February 1968 Harry Crowe, my former teacher, and his partner Doug Fisher were somewhere near the mark when in a Toronto *Telegram* column entitled "The Key to Trudeauism" they wrote that "when the historian Ramsay Cook looks into a mirror he sees Justice Minister Pierre Elliott Trudeau and when Mr. Trudeau looks he sees Professor Cook. It is Elie Kedourie, brilliant scholar of nationalism and the nation-state, who is holding the mirror."[8]

At Harvard, where we were both visiting professors in 1968, I told Professor Kedourie, whose wife came from Montreal, that the new prime minister of Canada admired his work. He was obviously pleased.

FIRST CONTACTS

By 1968 I had come to know Pierre Trudeau the person as well
as the writer. And as is so often the case, the person and the
writer struck me in contrasting ways. In April 1961 Jacqueline
Côté and Blair Neatby were married in Ottawa. I had become
their friend while doing research in the Public Archives every
summer during the late 1950s. Blair, like me a Saskatchewan
native with a keen interest in Quebec, had been appointed to
succeed McGregor Dawson as Mackenzie King's "official" biographer. Since he had for several years been courting Jacqueline, an archivist assigned to the King Papers, his return to
Ottawa from the University of British Columbia settled the
marriage question. One of the wedding guests was Pierre
Trudeau, a friend of Jacqueline's since his brief career in the
Privy Council Office in the early 1950s. Wearing a loden cape,
he swept into the wedding reception accompanied by Madeleine Gobeil, a quick-witted young professor of French literature at Carleton University ("the blonde," as some of his friends
called her, I later learned).

Moving among our fellow guests, we soon met – and soon
argued. As I now recall, Trudeau intervened in a discussion
that I was having with Fred Gibson over the newly announced
Liberal platform that Lester Pearson had described as "neither
Left nor Right, but Forward." This, I had written in the
Forum, was just the predictable Liberal quest for ambiguity.
Gibson, who knew my CCF sympathies (the NDP was still on
the horizon), disagreed and was seconded by Trudeau, who
thought the new program represented signs that the Liberals
were returning to reform. Trudeau was easy to argue with. He
listened and responded, never trying to dominate the conversation, always clear, always polite and friendly. It was a good

start to what would be nearly forty years of intermittent exchange. It seemed wonderfully academic, neither of us having any idea that it would lead anywhere beyond the moment. Since weddings are not a time for lengthy disputes, we soon returned to the festivities, though I hoped there would be a chance to resume our discussion. Later that year Trudeau contributed an essay, which cited both Acton and Mao Tse-tung, explaining (unsuccessfully it turned out) the virtues of decentralized federalism to other social democratic intellectuals in a volume called *Social Purpose for Canada*. In 1963 he supported his friend Charles Taylor's NDP candidacy in Mount Royal. Both the article and the political commitment pleased me.

TRANSLATIONS

Since early 1960 I had subscribed to *Cité libre*, whose editors were struggling to find a voice after Jean Lesage and the Liberals took office in Quebec on a platform that contained many planks that Trudeau and his friends had been advocating for a decade. The new government included the popular television journalist René Lévesque, whom the *citélibristes* knew well. Quite unexpectedly, the Quiet Revolution almost immediately unleashed a torrent of nationalist rhetoric, which, in its most radical version, advocated a separate, unilingual – and, in some cases socialist – Quebec. Trudeau was appalled. In April 1962, adapting Julien Benda, he fought back in "La nouvelle trahison des clercs." It bowled me over, not only because it rudely dissected separatism, but also because Trudeau applied the same sharp scalpel to nationalism in English Canada. He boldly sketched the case for a bilingual, polyethnic society, one that could be a model for other nations. I set about translating parts of it for the *Canadian Forum*. Naturally I asked his approval for my efforts, which he quickly gave. "If the *Canadian Forum* can use it, I should be pleased," he replied, while gently suggesting some improvements to the translation. One word in his text had utterly stumped my dictionaries and me. What, I asked, did *en Landerneau* mean? His reply revealed his remarkable command of English (and satire): "I don't know how to translate Landerneau. It is a little town in Brittany and the expression means to refer to things that happen in far-out, insignificant areas. If you think it would clear things up for English readers I suggest you replace the word by 'in this neck of the woods' or 'Toonerville' or something like that."[9] (Until he became a member of parliament, Trudeau's letters were always handwritten.) I opted for "Toonerville," which was right out of my childhood literary education. His official translator later chose "our own little part of the world," which muted the satire of Landerneau-Toonerville-Quebec.

The reaction to the translation of Trudeau's essay was curious. Even around the *Forum* editorial table in Lou and Kay Morris's kitchen, I felt a certain skepticism. Kildare Dobbs, Elizabeth Kilbourn, Milton Wilson, Bob Fulford, Jack Batten – these were Toronto people for whom Quebec was at best an unplumbable French mystery or, worse, a stereotype. Trudeau was not completely unknown outside Quebec, at least in small academic circles. He attended meetings of the Canadian Association of Economics and Political Science fairly regularly and in 1958 had published a prize-winning article entitled "Some Obstacles to Democracy in Quebec" in that association's journal. Yet he was something of an oddity. Even in Quebec, his nonconformity, his travels to the Soviet Union, China, and other unusual tourist destinations, to say nothing of his futile efforts to organize *rassemblements* of democrats to fight Duplessis, were often judged quixotic at best. In 1964 Professor

Gérard Bergeron, a distinguished Laval political scientist, told me that Trudeau was the most talented man of his generation but that he was a hopeless dilettante.

In English Canada in the early 1960s, Quebec was still viewed as a backwater ("Why waste your time translating editorials from *Le Devoir?*" one professor's wife asked me) and separatism a marginal fantasy. So why the fuss? One reader (who later became an admirer of René Lévesque) asked, after reading my translation, why Trudeau so hated English Canadians. Surely he was a separatist. The idea of an antinationalist proved harder to explain than separatism. But then the idea of French-language rights outside Quebec struck many as a replay of the story of King Canute. After all, North Americans spoke English; and Quebec, the *Globe and Mail* advised, should follow the Scottish example. (In those days, no one even dreamed that the Scots might find Quebec worthy of emulation!) In the academic world, protesting the U.S. war in Vietnam was all the rage and teach-ins were the order of the day, though the growing discontent of Quebecers was never a subject worth "teaching-in."

HAVE YOU READ MARX?

Yet students knew better, doubtless because their own organizations brought them face to face with student unrest and nationalist unrest in Quebec. In 1963 Richard Pope, a language student at the University of Toronto where I taught, invited me to act as faculty adviser to a student exchange known as the *Carabin* weekend. (The previous year, Mario Cardinal, a reporter for *Le Devoir*, and I had tried to tell the students what Quebec wanted.) This autumn our students again played host to students from the Université de Montréal, who chose Pierre

Trudeau as their academic guide. I enjoyed student conferences that had some intellectual substance, as this one promised to have. Seeing Trudeau again excited my interest even
more. The Toronto students invited Peter Gzowski of *Maclean's*
magazine to speak. Gzowski, one of the few English Canadian
journalists to take a serious interest in Quebec affairs, had recently written about Trudeau. As I remember it, Gzowski did
a good job at the conference, provoking questions from both
French- and English-speaking students. But mainly I remember Trudeau.

Now for the first time a professor (the new regime in Quebec had opened the doors to dissidents who had previously been
unwelcome), he seemed made for academic life in the 1960s.
He dressed casually, didn't smoke a pipe (or Gitanes either, for
that matter), treated the students as adults, and obviously
liked them. They responded readily to him and were left in no
doubt about his political ideas. The Montreal group included
a vocal separatist minority, the first I ever met. One gloried in
the name Michael McAndrew, proving that assimilation was a
two-way street. He professed great admiration for Cuba and
advocated an independent, French only, socialist, one-party
state. (McAndrew later worked for Radio-Canada, moving into
Lévesque's entourage after 1976.) Trudeau jousted with him
and other francophone students. At one point he even defended the monarchy, calling me to his aid – a desperate measure.
(Several years later, when asked by a journalist what he would
do if there was a public debate on the monarchy, he replied
that he would go skiing.) He told me of a student who, on the
trip to Toronto, had confessed his inability to understand sociologist Philippe Garigue's recently published *L'option politique pour le Québec.* "How many times did you read it?"
Trudeau asked. "Three," the student replied. "Have you read

Marx?" the professor demanded. "Or Mill? Or Tocqueville?" Triple negatives from the student. "Throw Garigue out the train window!" Trudeau advised. I remarked that I had read Garigue and was also left puzzled about his option. I did not admit that I had tried it twice.

What struck me most about Pierre Trudeau that weekend was his relaxed manner with the students – argumentative but courteous. Although I had been in academic life nearly six years and greatly enjoyed teaching, I was still stiff and insecure, not knowing quite what a professor's relationship should be with these slightly-younger-than-me young people. Even more, I noticed how much at ease Trudeau was with himself. His independence of mind gave him a freedom that I had seen in few people, even in the university world. He was, as we had learned to say, utterly "inner-directed." That impressed me not only then but afterwards too – to the end of his life. It made him a provocative intellectual and teacher. As things turned out, this was also his greatest strength as a political leader. It may also have been his main weakness as a politician. He needed no backpatting, he asked no favours. He never quite understood that both backpatting and favours are essential politician's tools. "I'm not a lonely guy," he explained when I once told him that if he was at a loose end any evening when the students were on their own, he was welcome to come home with me. That, too, revealed the kind of leader he would become. Intellect, charm, self-discipline, independence, wit, a unique personal magnetism: *le style, c'est l'homme même*. All those characteristics were there to see in 1963, all pointing to a brilliant academic future for Professor Trudeau.

Student exchanges further stimulated my interest in Quebec, now my principal teaching responsibility. My interests were both historical and contemporary, and by the fall of 1963 I feared that the jurisdictional struggle between Quebec and Ottawa over the terms of the Canada Pension Plan might lead to a fatal breach in Confederation. So I joined some concerned students (Peter Dembowski, a witty professor of French married to a French Canadian, was the only other professor to participate) in a march on Queen's Park to urge Premier John Robarts to take a conciliatory position at that weekend's federal-provincial conference in Quebec City. Our hope was that we would get the attention of both the Ontario delegation and the Quebec media. But on the day of our march, 22 November 1963, President John F. Kennedy was assassinated, an event that left little space for our march even on the back pages of the press. Eventually, of course, a compromise Canada-Quebec pension plan was established. I rejoiced, but I later concluded that the short-term peace unintentionally contributed to Quebec's increasing demands for greater autonomy, especially since the funds from the provincial pension fund, deposited in the Caisse de dépot, could be used to promote economic independence.

INTO COMBAT

By 1964 the noise of the Quiet Revolution could be heard from coast to coast, though not everyone was listening. Pierre Trudeau and six of his friends had already concluded that the sound and fury of nationalist rhetoric in Quebec signified, if not nothing, then certainly the wrong message to Canadians everywhere. Over several months, they drew up a document calling for a rejection of political slogans in favour of concrete solutions to specific problems. Nationalism, French or English Canadian, they contended, was a mere smokescreen for middle-class interests, offering no practical solutions to real social and economic problems. These ideas certainly appealed to me.

When Marc Lalonde, whom at that time I did not know, called me in April 1964 proposing that *Cité libre* and the *Forum* jointly publish the Trudeau group's manifesto, I accepted the offer with alacrity. Lalonde, unknowingly preparing to become Trudeau's principal secretary, was then in Lester Pearson's office, having moved there after a stint with Davie Fulton, the Conservative minister of justice. Trudeau then came on the phone. We exchanged some pleasantries and I promised to fix up matters with the *Forum*. Trudeau told me that the group had hoped to interest *Maclean's* and *Le magazine Maclean* but had been told the manifesto was too academic. What a misjudgment! In May the *Manifeste pour une politique fonctionnelle* appeared in both publications, demonstrating among other things the determination of Trudeau and his friends to spread their federalist and pragmatic ideas in both French and English Canada.[10] Of the seven authors, only Trudeau and Lalonde eventually entered federal politics, and this document may have been a step in that direction – though none of us, neither the members of the Pléiade nor I, thought so at the time. Since Michael Pitfield did the English translation and I picked it up from him at Government House in Ottawa, where he was working for the governor general, the nucleus of Trudeau's future team was beginning to fall into place. The published manifesto attracted a small amount of media attention but then dropped from sight and, unfortunately, has since been largely ignored by Trudeau's biographers.

That same spring a young man named Jean-Pierre Fournier asked if I would help the Canadian Union of Students organize a national seminar on "A New Concept of Confederation," to be held at Université Laval in August. He told me that Professor Jacques-Yvan Morin, a professor of law at the Université de Montréal, would act as the other faculty adviser. I readily agreed, without realizing that I was about to experience the workings of what in those days was called associate-states, an early version of sovereignty-association. It was from Professor Morin, who had an astonishingly British accent, acquired at Cambridge, that I learned he was to choose the French Canadian speakers; the English Canadians would be my responsibility. In practice this meant that when I urged him to include Pierre Elliott Trudeau on his list, he firmly rejected the idea on the grounds that Trudeau's views were too well known.

As it turned out, so were those of his two selections. The first was Professor Michel Brunet, whom I had known since the mid-fifties when we both spent many hot summer days doing research at the Public Archives in Ottawa. He had recently written a constitutional brief for the St-Jean-Baptiste Society (Montreal section) advocating a new confederation of equal nations. The second name was also familiar to me: Jean-Marc Léger, an editorialist with *Le Devoir*, who had long advocated a new form of federation modelled, as André Laurendeau had explained it to me, on the dual Austro-Hungarian Empire! I soon learned that Morin himself had worked out a set of ideas on constitutional reform that called for an association of two equal nations. He was not a separatist, he later told me, because he wanted to protect the rights of francophone minorities outside Quebec and the English in Quebec. (Some casual remarks on an evening stroll left me with the clear impression that the rights of people such as Mordecai Richler concerned him rather less.)

Morin may have thought that I, a federalist, also had chosen a common front – picking English-speaking federalists. It didn't seem quite that way to me. The two I had selected were the historian W.L. Morton, an outspoken centralist, and the political scientist Donald Smiley, a decentralist. Morton favoured language duality, while Smiley, coming from British Columbia, looked skeptically on the concept. So I thought the students would get a variety of English Canadian opinion. For after-dinner entertainment, each of us chose a politician. Morin, true to form, suggested Pierre Laporte, a minister in the Lesage government who advocated a special status for Quebec that verged on sovereignty. Thinking that someone had to speak for those Quebecers who favoured some version of the existing federal system (at the time easily the majority), I suggested Maurice Sauvé, a leftish member of the Pearson cabinet. Although I had chosen a French Canadian, Morin did not object.

The participants from outside Quebec certainly went home with the impression that Quebec had finished with the existing federal system. The Quebec students, like the Quebec speakers, left no doubt about that. When Pierre Marois, then the president of the Université de Montréal students' association (and after 1976 a Parti Québécois cabinet minister), eloquently voiced his *indépendantiste* convictions, he seemed to speak for most of the Quebec students. Only the rare Acadian student dissented. Soon after the conference, the Quebec students decided to form their own separate organization, the Union générale des étudiants du Quebec (UGEQ), as if to prepare for the future.[11]

Returning to Ottawa, where I was enjoying my first sabbatical leave, I was disappointed and somewhat depressed. There had been no real exchange of views among the students, I thought, because Morin had succeeded in establishing a single voice for Quebec, and any deviation, if tolerated, required a good deal of courage. In an effort to clarify my own thoughts, I wrote a long article examining what I believed were the various options that Quebecers were considering for their future relations with the rest of Canada. "Quebec and Confederation: A Look at Some Current Proposals" appeared over several days in the *Montreal Star*, whose editor, my friend George Ferguson, had occasionally provided me with a chance to reach Quebec readers. Pierre Trudeau, on his return from "attending the British elections," as he put it, wrote to express his agreement with my analysis, especially my negative assessment of the associate-states concept. He wondered about publishing a translation in *Cité libre*.[12] In the end, that did not work out, but I already had an alternative proposal.

At the Quebec City student conference, I had been surprised at the lengths to which Michel Brunet had gone to talk with the students and especially to press his ideas on them. Both forceful and jolly, he had advanced a simple concept that had long been familiar to me from his historical writings. Canada, he argued, was not one nation but two: "Canadiens et Canadiens." Unnaturally joined with the Canadians in a single federal state, the Canadien minority, misled by their leaders into believing that federalism protected their rights, was always left with the crumbs and was threatened with inevitable assimilation. The Conquest, Brunet contended, had settled the fate of the French Canadians, a fate that could only be avoided if Quebec increasingly became a national state. Given the dominance of majorities over minorities, only three things counted in history, he told the students: "first, numbers; second, numbers; third, numbers" – a line used by a professor to open Denys Arcand's film *Le déclin de l'Empire américain*. Brunet's message was a maddenly pessimistic one, especially for the young. He had adapted most of these ideas from his reclusive colleague Maurice Séguin and from Guy Frégault, a Université de Montréal historian who moved into the Quebec public service after 1960. ("Séguin sçie, Frégault écrit, et Brunet crie," the Université de Montréal students quipped.) Once back in

Ottawa I sat down and read all of Brunet's writings, extracted his principal ideas, and composed an essay arguing that his
historical vision was seriously warped by his nationalist faith.

When Trudeau read the manuscript, which I had sent for his
comments, he wrote a complimentary, analytical letter to me.
He suggested a few improvements and urged me to publish it
simultaneously in *Cité libre* and the *Forum*. Then he added a
revealing sentence: "It casts a new, historical light on the nationalism of René L. and the separatists. And I think this light
is, in reality, more devastating than our (Ryan, Pelletier, Taylor, myself) philosophical or political arguments. I like the tone,
too, which is not too sarcastic or impassioned. In this too, the
article will be a welcome one in our present polemics."[13] This
reference to René Lévesque seemed curious, since he was still
a cabinet minister in Lesage's Liberal government. But Trudeau
was already convinced that his old acquaintance's repeated attacks on the Canadian federal system, together with his insistence that the Quebec state was the national state of French
Canadians, would ultimately lead him into the separatist fold.
In this he was right; he was pointing directly to the relationship between the basic ideas of the quasi-separatist historian
and the nationalist politician. (Brunet, who had a healthy ego,
once answered my question about his influence on Lévesque
by saying that it was obvious – he had seen Lévesque reading
one of his books on the picket line during the famous 1959
Radio-Canada producers' strike!) In January my article appeared in *Cité libre* and soon afterwards in the *Tamarack Review* – an odd article for a literary magazine; odder still, it won
a medal as the best scholarly article published in 1965. Michel
Brunet did not object to the piece. Jacques-Yvan Morin, on the
other hand, wrote protesting that I had unfairly accused

Brunet of *passe-passe* – sleight of hand.[14] True enough I suppose, since Brunet was a nationalist.

The Brunet piece, I think, cemented our friendship. Trudeau realized that my interest in Quebec was based on considerable knowledge, though he urged me not to waste too much time on the famous "national question." This, "after all, is not as important as your real work," he said, adding that the subject, "under other pens, is becoming such a bore."[15] He believed that being a scholar was far more important and promised more durable results than polemics and journalism. That, of course, had been his message to Quebec intellectuals, whom he thought were obsessed with the national question; that was the "new treason." He would often gently remind me of my proper calling, draw me into historical discussions, dropping a line or two from Thucydides. I loved the discussions and ignored the advice – or rather, I tried to be both historian and engaged intellectual. The balance was not easy to keep; the essays I wrote often had an immediate impact, but their shelf life was probably more limited than my strictly scholarly works. But essay writing suited my impatient temperament and (I convinced myself) contributed to the public debate.

Trudeau knew, of course, that I ignored his advice, for in the autumn of 1964 I began writing a weekly column in *Le Devoir* on the invitation of Claude Ryan (who translated most of these pieces himself). I had come to know Ryan during the previous year as we both hit the conference road offering our then similar answers to the famous question, "What does Quebec want?" – the answer being a more decentralized, bilingual federation. He also knew me from my *Forum* writings and translations, and perhaps through André Laurendeau, whom I had met and liked very much when he lectured at the University of Toronto in the spring of 1962. Being, as he said, a night person, Laurendeau had readily accepted an invitation from Eleanor and me to join us at our Madison Avenue flat for a drink after the lecture, and this led to a long evening of conversation. On returning from a trip to the bathroom, Laurendeau asked with a straight face, "What is this strange Anglo-Saxon custom I have discovered?" Since we looked puzzled, he laughed and said, "Your PHD diploma is hanging in the toilet!" Subsequently, I wrote a sketch of his ideas for the *Forum,* based on his recently published *La crise de la conscription 1942.*

When Laurendeau accepted the co-chairmanship of the Royal Commission on Bilingualism and Biculturalism, Claude Ryan assumed the editorial chair at *Le Devoir.* I knew that Trudeau, Laurendeau, and Ryan were all federalists but also that they assessed nationalism differently. These differences would grow over the next few years. Trudeau systematically criticized the preliminary report of the B and B Commission. I commented favourably, drawing a revealing letter from Laurendeau explaining the use of the word "crisis" in the report.[16] (When in 1968 Ryan opposed Trudeau's candidacy for the Liberal Party leadership, it was for reasons that were probably shared but not stated by Laurendeau – both favoured an undefined "special status" for Quebec. Since I supported Trudeau, my relations with Ryan became very strained. Laurendeau died suddenly in the spring of 1968, so I never had to choose between him and Trudeau, though I had, of course, already done so.)

Meanwhile, when in 1964 I agreed to write the column in Montreal's nationalist daily, it was for several reasons. One, of course, was simply ego. I was a longtime admirer of the famous newspaper and also of its founder Henri Bourassa, and the thought of reaching a French-language audience was irresistible. Moreover, having done some research on the newspaper's history, I knew that Bourassa had always planned to have at least one English-language contributor. His first choice had been John Ewart, whose views on both Canada's place in the British Empire and on French-language educational and language rights were close to Bourassa's. That plan had never been fulfilled, for reasons that I had not been able to discover, and to help fulfill it fifty or so years late appealed to me very much. My other reason for taking up the offer was a conviction, not yet fully shared by Trudeau, that French-English relations were in deep crisis – the Laurendeau view.

I had followed the French-language press avidly for several years, and my contacts with French Canadian journalists and scholars – the Canadian Union of Students conference in 1964 and the Canadian Historical Association meeting in Quebec City in 1965 – had convinced me that underneath the changes and the noisy demands for more changes in Quebec was a powerful, uncontrolled thrust towards separation. *Épanouissement* (flowering), the catchword of those days, might produce unexpected fruit. I thought that part of the problem was a serious lack of knowledge in English Canada of French Canada and vice versa. My editorials and translations in the *Forum* and my teaching at the university were designed to fill some of the gaps in English Canada. Writing in *Le Devoir* opened a route to French Canada. The liberal naiveté of this belief occasionally occurred to me, but I easily set it aside. My books and articles found a readership, and I always had lots of students, but whether anything in particular followed from that is hard to say.

Claude Ryan told me that my articles in his paper often drew comment. One came from a disgruntled reader who claimed that my contributions, coming after the award of a prize to a

newsboy with an English name, was a further sign of the sub-
version of the nationalist newspaper by its Irish editor! And
Jacques Ferron, the nationalist novelist and founder of the
Rhinoceros Party, wrote directly to say in an amusingly denun-
ciatory fashion that my contributions were just another act in
an already stale English Canadian *opéra bouffe*. I was flattered
even to be read by this author, though I admired his sister Mar-
celle's paintings more than his novels. Trudeau wrote a complimentary letter, suggesting that I had an attentive university
readership. Characteristically, he had especially enjoyed a column in which I had pointed out that despite all the talk about
Confederation in Quebec, no Quebec historian had bothered
to write a documented study of the subject: "I hope you are not
burning all your midnight oil getting these things done! Save
some energy for the festive season, which I hope will be a merry
and peaceful one for you and your family."[17]

PIERRE GOES TO OTTAWA

Although I was unaware of it, there had been talks between
Trudeau and some of his friends with some Quebec Liberals before the federal election of 1963. But Lester Pearson's decision
to accept nuclear warheads for the Bomarc missiles stationed
in Canada had abruptly ended those talks. In a fierce polemic
entitled "Pearson ou l'abdication de l'ésprit," Trudeau had
charged the Liberal leader with unashamed opportunism and
with sacrificing his reputation as a peacemaker. Two years later,
with his friends Jean Marchand and Gérard Pelletier, Pierre
Trudeau made his leap of faith. "You can well imagine," he
wrote to me, "that my decision to enter politics on the Liberal
side was a difficult one."[18] Although the Liberals did not much

want him, the three men had decided to go as a package – or not at all. (Ironically, it was René Lévesque, feeling isolated in the Lesage cabinet, who had recommended this strategy.) Since I was a member of the New Democratic Party and had often hoped that Trudeau would join my party, this decision disappointed me. But at the same time I knew that the NDP in Quebec was a lost cause and that federalism needed strong defenders from that province, especially since the Pearson government seemed increasingly muddled in its reactions to Quebec constitutional demands.

Pearson seemed to believe, perhaps drawing on his experience as a diplomat, that every problem could be solved by compromise. At least, that struck me as the essence of the amorphous phrase "cooperative federalism," coined to disguise a policy vacuum by such people as Jean-Luc Pepin, a political scientist turned Liberal politician, who should have known better. By 1965 I had concluded that while the Lesage Liberals were as unclear as anyone else about exactly what Quebec wanted, they nevertheless would continue to expand their demands indefinitely and would take everything they could get, testing the limits of "cooperation." Someone had to call Quebec's bluff, and Pierre Trudeau seemed to be the person. So his departure to Ottawa as a Liberal – easily elected in Mount Royal – was welcome in this important sense. And it certainly promised to be a good show to watch.

During the next two years, as Trudeau advanced from parliamentary assistant to Pearson, to minister of justice (appointments that displayed either Pearson's ability to forgive or his misunderstanding of Trudeau's views), I watched with interest. Geoffrey Pearson, whom I had met through Blair and Jacqueline Neatby, told me his father was struck by Trudeau's discipline: he regularly pressed the prime minister to stop flying by the seat of his pants and to adopt a plan, a strategy. Trudeau obviously made his intellectual weight felt on the constitutional front very early. By 1966 Mitchell Sharp, the minister of finance, effectively dropped the "opting-out" policy which Pepin and others had devised to allow Quebec a wider range of autonomy within federal programs. Trudeau saw this as "special status" by stealth, and so did I.

In these years of his apprenticeship we kept up our occasional contacts. In May 1966 we both attended a curious conference at Glendon College in Toronto convened by EPIC, the Exchange for Political Ideas in Canada. Des Sparham, its organizer, was an Englishman who had worked to create "New Party Clubs" as a prelude to the founding of the NDP. Now he had moved on to try to establish a sort of Fabian Society, which he may also have seen as a left-wing activists' meeting place that might eventually nurture a Liberal-NDP alliance. The speakers at the conference were drawn from both parties, and there may have been some tentative talk among them about unity. When I first saw Trudeau, I remarked that he looked no more like a politician than ever. He replied that I didn't look any more like a professor.

The conference was interesting enough, especially because in addition to Pierre Trudeau I met Marc Lalonde again and had a chance to talk to both Walter Gordon and Doug Fisher. (Walter Gordon was wonderfully witty: entering Escott Reid's handsomely appointed apartment at Glendon College he remarked dryly that things weren't too bad for college principals these days. Reid muttered something about his former ambassadorial rank.) The conference outcome was certainly a disappointment to those who had hoped to promote the unity of the left. I don't know if Trudeau was one of those. He certainly would not have had much difficulty accepting NDP social and foreign policies. But he considered the party's "two nations" doctrine to be totally confused and dangerous. His friend Eugene Forsey had departed from the NDP on that issue, and I would soon follow. The NDP, guided by Michael Oliver and Charles Taylor, and anxious to win support in Quebec, was in the process of making a fatal error by attempting to appeal to Quebec nationalists. These were often left-leaning francophone intellectuals who shared the NDP's commitment to social democracy but in the final analysis were much more attracted to some form of Quebec independence. My commitment to social democracy was internationalist not nationalist, and that also was Trudeau's view. As the NDP moved to accommodate the Michel Chartrands, Jacques-Yvan Morins, and Pierre Vadeboncoeurs, it lost the Pierre Trudeaus, Jean Marchands, and Gérard Pelletiers. In this zero-sum game, the NDP ended with zero.

Often I tried to explain to NDP intellectuals what I saw as the problem, but to no avail. After one vigorous exchange with the brilliant political scientist Gad Horowitz, he wrote, "Trudeau is still fighting *Duplessis* and you are still fighting the *Orange Lodge*. They are both dead (but I fear a little bit of the latter still lives in McNaught)."[19] Horowitz's quip revealed a misunderstanding, and in some cases an intentional distortion, of Trudeau's position that was typical of many francophone and anglophone nationalists. He was not fighting Duplessis, who was indeed dead. Rather, he was combatting the ideology that had made Duplessis and his successors possible – nationalism. Trudeau knew that the distinction often drawn by nationalists between "good" nationalism (mine) and "bad" nationalism (yours) did not stand up to serious analysis. Nationalism in all its manifestations stood for ethnic homogeneity and cultural conformity. Modern, progressive societies were nourished by ethnic plurality and cultural hybridity. Concluding a 1961 essay entitled "L'aliénation nationaliste," Trudeau wrote, "Open the frontiers, this people is dying of asphyxiation."[20] In 1964, as I saw my left-wing friends being seduced by nationalism, I argued in a study of nationalism in Quebec that "nationalism can release creative energies in a people. It can also be destructive and reactionary because it enforces conformity where individualism and pluralism are necessary if society is to progress."[21] If Horowitz had thought through his clever comment about our mutual friend Ken McNaught, he would have understood his own error. Just as McNaught's left-wing nationalism revealed its "Orange" – English Canadian Protestant – ethnic roots, so the "new" Quebec nationalism of the 1960s had its source in the ethnic ideology of *la survivance* that Duplessis had manipulated so successfully. Duplessis and the Orange Lodge were both dead. Nationalism in the 1960s remained alive and well, and was threatening to return Quebec to its "wigwam mentality" and to divide the country. Consequently, Trudeau continued the battle. Horowitz soon moved on to the study of Hegel.

During centennial year, Trudeau's public profile gradually blossomed. His appointment as minister of justice ensured that his constitutional principles – which permitted no special status for any province – became government policy. But before he had an opportunity to explain this policy publicly, he devoted himself to legislating substantial reforms to the divorce law and the removal of homosexuality from the Criminal Code. Then, in July, when President Charles de Gaulle so dramatically proclaimed "Vive le Québec libre!" during his visit to Montreal, Trudeau joined other Quebec cabinet ministers in pressing Lester Pearson to declare that the French president's pronouncement was "unacceptable." In contrast to the more conciliatory minister of external affairs, Paul Martin, Trudeau and Marchand were absolutely firm in their insistence that de Gaulle be left in no doubt about the Canadian government's diplomatic anger.

By the time of de Gaulle's declaration, the Quebec government, now back in the hands of the Union Nationale, led by Daniel Johnson, had been pressing for increased powers in foreign affairs. This kind of demand made the concept of "special status" increasingly clear. It was what later became known as *étapisme,* or step-by-step independence. I participated in several television programs, including one with Paul Gérin-Lajoie, the provincial Liberals' constitutional expert, where the jurisdictional issue was discussed. These exchanges convinced me that my friend the minister of justice held the only logical position: outright opposition to any attempt to identify the Quebec nation with the Quebec state. (Although I was not acquainted with him, Eric Kierans took the trouble to let me know that he agreed with me and not with his former cabinet colleague. Later that year Kierans played a major role in the constitutional battle that led to René Lévesque's departure from the Quebec Liberal Party.)

Trudeau's goal was to force Quebecers to choose between the only two logical options: a federal system, where all provinces exercised the same powers, or Quebec independence. Any middle position that granted Quebec a special status because of its claim to be a "national" state would gradually but inexorably lead to separation. Trudeau had little respect for those intellectuals, of either language group, who disguised their refusal to choose behind a smokescreen of undefined slogans such as "une province pas comme les autres," "particular status," and "special status."

MY PARTY ... WRONG

At its 1967 national convention in Toronto, the NDP moved from its 1961 position, which had called for recognition that Canada was composed of "two nations" – one French Canadian and one English Canadian – to support an undefined "special status" for Quebec. I attended that convention as an observer. Watching the debate over Quebec's status, I became convinced that virtually no one, including Tommy Douglas, had any specific understanding of the confused concept that was being adopted. Moreover, the repeated attacks on the Liberal minister of justice for his supposed rigidity and anti-Quebec attitude struck me as the worst sort of partisanship – nothing more than thinly veiled charges of betrayal against a former sympathizer. In an effort to convince my fellow NDPers of the error of their ways and to explain and defend the position of the minister of justice, I wrote an article for the *Globe and Mail* arguing that the NDP had slipped into a constitutional quagmire that would be its undoing.

The article, "What's Special about the NDP's Status for Quebec?," was hard hitting, condemning my party's latest attempt to formulate a policy that would attract support in Quebec (see appendix 1). I commented on the convention debate and analysed parliamentary speeches on the constitution by NDP members. My point was to reveal the party's apparent ignorance of what the phrase "special status" meant in Quebec, something radically different from what the NDP's anglophone leaders appeared to be talking about. In the process, I set out Trudeau's position and defended it: "The latest NDP proclamation on Canadian federalism indicates that the party still sees federalism as something to circumvent, rather than one of the prime necessities of Canadian existence." And I concluded: "Canada is a difficult country to govern, it has often been remarked. The NDP appears to believe that it is a difficult country to govern because it has a federal system. The truth, and it is a truth which Mr. Trudeau has recognized, is that Canada has a federal system because it is a difficult country to govern."[22]

What would the party's reaction be to a member who attacked both the party's policy and its leadership? It turned out to be quite mild. Charles Taylor, perhaps at the party's request, sent a long (and I thought confused) reply, which the *Globe* showed me but did not publish and which my NDP friend Ken McNaught pronounced as "gobbedlygook." There was no immediate reaction from other friends in the NDP, most of whom took little interest in constitutional issues. Nor, for that matter, was there in Quebec. There was, however, an immediate reaction from the minister of justice, whom I had, about a month earlier, congratulated on straightening the Liberals out on constitutional matters. Not surprisingly, he expressed his agreement with my *Globe* article and remarked that it might "initiate some serious thinking on the whole question in English and French Canada."[23] Later that year, when Trudeau published his splendid collection of essays, *Le fédéralisme et la société canadienne-française*, he referred in his introduction to my essay as *un essentiel travail de démystification*. On the title page of the copy he sent me, he wrote (I would say "flatteringly," if Pierre ever flattered): "À Ramsay Cook, allié courageux et infatigable dans notre combat pour le fédéralisme et la société canadienne-française." And he sealed the pact in closing, "avec beaucoup d'amitié Pierre E.T."

Interestingly, in his letter commenting on my critique of special status, he raised another matter. He asked if I had any ideas that might be useful in trying to convince the United States to alter its stand "even a little" on Vietnam. Before signing the letter, he appended a handwritten sentence: "On this point, I have some cause to believe that Peking is doing its best to prevent Hanoi from reaching any kind of agreement with Washington." These remarks did not surprise me, for Trudeau had always had an informed interest in international affairs and a deep concern about the possibility of nuclear war. But for the primacy of the constitutional debate, he probably would have preferred to have the External Affairs portfolio rather than Justice. Unfortunately, I had no brilliant ideas to offer, other than to repeat the suggestion which I and other Toronto professors, led by Anton Kuerti and John Polanyi, had already made in a petition to the Pearson government: State Canada's opposition to the war more forthrightly. But neither Prime Minister Pearson nor External Affairs Minister Paul Martin, we discovered, had any desire to face the wrath of President Johnson again!

A few days later another letter arrived, this time from Marc Lalonde, now Pearson's principal secretary. After telling me that he admired my *Globe* piece, he expressed a more far-reaching concern than I had ever heard from Trudeau. "One of my big worries currently," he wrote, "is the problem of the alienation of the Quebec F.C. intellectuals vis-à-vis the federal government. I am still wondering whether this is a passing phenomenon that our current reforms at the federal level will eventually cure or whether this is something we will have to live with forever. In the latter case, I think there is good cause for worry about the future of Quebec and of Canada." He ended with a comment that reflected my own particular and, I thought, nonpartisan preoccupation: "We may be heading for a basic confrontation in the next few years and the federal parties have a very heavy responsibility of public education in Quebec about federalism and Canada. Will they act responsibly or will they just play politics with the constitution? The latest NDP exercise is not a source of encouragement."[24]

Lalonde was in touch again late in October, saying that he would like to talk with me if he came to Toronto for the Confederation for Tomorrow Conference, which Premier John Robarts of Ontario had called for November. He seemed a bit more upbeat. "I think things are beginning to move in the right direction," he remarked, "but we must prevent (?) all the same the English-speaking Canadians from falling again into complacency."[25] Lalonde was only an observer at the Robarts conference, the federal government having refused to attend a meeting convened by a province. We watched some of it together, intrigued and distressed by the ease with which Daniel Johnson succeeded in charming his counterparts into believing that *Égalité ou indépendance*, the title of his recent book, could be achieved without seriously disturbing anyone. (I, too, had been charmed by Johnson. In a CBC radio interview that I had done with him some months earlier, he had offered to translate one of my books into French if I would agree to turn his into English!) Of course, Premier Robarts, who was never as sleepy as he regularly looked, kept the conference to generalities. But one goal was achieved. Until now the federal government, on Trudeau's insistence, had refused to call a general constitutional conference, on the grounds that it would be premature. This stand could no longer be sustained against the provinces, the opposition parties, and much of the press, especially in Quebec. It was not long before Pearson announced that a federal-provincial conference on the constitution would be convened in early February 1968.

My own position on the revision of the constitution had clarified. For six years I had believed that no major changes were necessary, that Quebec could be accommodated by the kind of ad hoc arrangements that fell under the open-ended concept of "cooperative federalism." But the NDP's adoption of "special status," and more particularly a remarkable student conference at Glendon College in November 1967 entitled "Quebec: Year Eight," forced me to choose a more precise option. As the closing speaker at a conference that had heard many of Quebec's foremost luminaries, I made my declaration. Having listened as Jean-Luc Pepin, the smiling genius of "cooperative federalism," debated René Lévesque, who had recently taken the first steps towards forming a new party advocating sovereignty-association, I told the audience that only two possible roads to equality for French Canadians existed. One was independence, the other was a revised federal system making "room for French Canadians in Canada as a whole." I continued, "We have to begin to work together to build a more just society in which French Canadians would increasingly share power rather than just the symbols of power."[26] My own choice was obvious.

TWO

LIBERAL MALGRÉ LUI

Et si l'on excepte Laurier, je ne vois pas un seul Canadien français
depuis d'un demi-siècle dont la présence au sien du Cabinet federal
puisse être considérée comme indispensable à l'histoire du Canada.
                    PIERRE ELLIOTT TRUDEAU, 1962

PETITIONING PIERRE

Before the federal-provincial conference met, Lester Pearson
announced that it would be his last. He intended to retire, he
told Canadians in December 1967, and had asked that a leadership convention be called for the first week in April the following year. The long list of potential candidates ambitious to
succeed Pearson did not include any French Canadian, though
Jean Marchand was certainly a possibility. In my mind, or
imagination, the name of Pierre Trudeau immediately surfaced.
I soon learned that I was not alone in this fantasy. I urged him
to go for the job, and I let Marc Lalonde know what I was up
to. He was up to the same thing, though his position in Pearson's office forced him to be discreet. But then Lalonde never
needed or wanted the limelight; he always chose effectiveness
over publicity, a characteristic that made him Trudeau's most
valuable political ally and trusted friend. Lalonde's response to
me was immediate. "Keep urging Pierre," he wrote in mid-
December. "I think he can be convinced if we can assure him
that he can have support across the country. As at present he

has not said he would *never* consider it under any condition. Anyway it would be a mistake for Pierre to commit himself before the constitutional conference, early in February." In the meantime, there were things that could be done. Lalonde suggested that maybe in January I could circulate a petition to "about 100 top professors across Canada," and perhaps others could be asked to write Pierre and to keep his name before the public.[1]

By the time the Christmas party season had arrived, the main subject of conversation in this highly politicized time – the 1960s – was the Liberal leadership contest. Most people in my academic and artistic circles, whether Liberal or NDP, were bored by the emerging names: Martin, Hellyer, Winters, MacEachen, Green, Turner, and Sharp. One night in a conversation with Mashel Teitelbaum, a marvellously unconventional painter friend, and his politically astute wife Ethel, I revealed my Trudeau fantasy. Mashel, his dark, deep-set eyes shining, pronounced the idea "fantastic." Ethel enthusiastically endorsed it too. Her response was the important one, because she had both the political skills and the Liberal connections which neither Mashel nor I had. She worked for Donald Macdonald, the ambitious young Liberal MP for Rosedale, a man on the left of his party. Our unlikely trio would start a petition and, I supposed, Ethel would speak to Don Macdonald. Since I thought that others with a higher profile among Liberals might be more effective in gathering names, I recruited Bill Kilbourn, an historian and an active Liberal. And I sent copies of the petition to friends in other parts of the country. We went to work over the Christmas season and discovered an encouraging response.

The signed petitions went to Trudeau, so for the most part I have only my memory to rely on. The signatories were certainly not only "top professors," or top anythings, since people wrote from many parts of the country asking us to add their names. But some were high profile. Bill Kilbourn liked to tell the story of getting Pierre Berton to sign at the annual Christmas party hosted by the publisher John Gray. The story was true, but Bill failed to mention that he didn't collect any other names. One scrap of paper I still have reads, "Pierre Elliott Trudeau is a good shit (merde.)" The signatories were J. Callwood, P. Gzowski, T. Frayne, Jenny Gzowski, and Barbara Frum.[2] It wasn't clear whether they thought they were describing the qualifications of a future prime minister or just practising their French. Many signatories wanted to know what else they could do. I had no answer.

By January 1968 the Trudeau campaign began to move in Toronto and, though I was unaware of it, even more so in Ottawa and Montreal. In Ottawa, Eddie Rubin, Trudeau's executive assistant, had started a skeleton organization, and in Montreal the Quebec wing of the Liberal Party was searching for a French Canadian to enter the race. Over Christmas I had suggested to my neighbour John Gray, president of Macmillan of Canada, that his company publish a translation of Trudeau's recent book. He agreed, but since Trudeau was still largely unknown for anything but his often casual dress and his legal reforms, Jim Bacque, the editor of Macmillan, decided that an introduction by a high-profile figure was needed. His thoughts turned to Pierre Berton and Peter Newman, but he finally settled on my friend Professor John T. Saywell, who was then host of a popular weekly CBC-TV public affairs program. The choice seemed a good one, but it apparently surprised Trudeau. One day in mid-January he phoned to say that he had wanted the introduction written by either me or Don Smiley, scholars with whose view he was familiar. I assured him that Saywell would do a good job and had asked me to look at his essay once it was written. The minister of justice seemed satisfied, and I returned to shovelling my sidewalk. Ironically, when the book finally appeared not long before the Liberal leadership convention, Trudeau was better known than Saywell, and it soon hit the bestseller list. It had certainly never occurred to me that *Federalism and the French Canadians* would help make Pierre prime minister. I had wanted it translated so that my students could read it.

Something else happened that January. I received an unexpected invitation from the Toronto Businessmen's Liberal Association to join Harry Crowe, a York professor and journalist associated with the NDP, and Serrell Hillman, the Toronto correspondent of *Time* magazine, in a discussion of the leadership campaign. Harry Crowe was mocking and sarcastic, congratulating the Liberals for recognizing their need for a leader. The *Time* man simply surveyed the field, remarking that if Pierre Trudeau entered the race it would at least be exciting. I took the opportunity to advocate rather than satirize or analyse. The noncandidate, Pierre Trudeau, was by far the best choice, I said. He had a brilliant mind, and his enemies, the nationalists in Quebec, were the best ones a federal politician could have. Above all, he met the requirements of Ward's law perfectly. Norman Ward, a Saskatchewan political scientist and humorist, had once proved – tongue-in-cheek – that prime ministerial longevity varied in proportion to marital status and family size. Bachelorhood explained the success of Mackenzie King. Trudeau, I pointed out, was a bachelor. I was listened to politely and got a few chuckles but, I think, few converts.

After the meeting my MP, Ian Wahn, told me that all Trudeau had was brains, and brains could be hired. He was for Paul Hellyer. But later, during the federal election that followed

Trudeau's leadership win, Wahn gladly appeared on his campaign literature with Trudeau's photo. In a campaign leaflet passed out in his riding, Wahn wrote, "In Mr. Trudeau, the Liberal party has a team leader of great intellectual ability, who thinks clearly, who says exactly what he thinks and acts decisively."[3] I remembered saying something along those lines. Not long after the election, Wahn took me to lunch at the National Club, during which he hinted that I might put in a good word on his behalf with the PM (As the saying goes, there's no such thing as a free lunch.) I didn't. Charles Caccia was my candidate for cabinet, though he never asked for my help. (He remained what he liked to call a permanent "Trudeau dinosaur," and so did I.) A few years later, Arthur Gelber, a Liberal and a generous patron of the arts who had attended the businessmen's lunch meeting, described me as the discoverer of Pierre Trudeau. "Only in the sense that Columbus discovered America, I replied. Trudeau, like America, had always been there."

Again like America after Columbus, new discoverers of Pierre Trudeau began to arrive in growing numbers. As the February federal-provincial conference on the constitution called by Pearson approached, media attention focused on the minister of justice, especially since he was rumoured to be considering a run at the Liberal leadership. The conference made Trudeau an almost instant national figure. More important, he demonstrated the impact he had personally made on the Pearson government's approach to constitutional change. He presented as government policy his proposal that a charter of rights, including language rights, be entrenched in the constitution. This was an idea that he had first launched in an article in *Maclean's* in February 1964 and had explained in detail in a lengthy paper at a conference of professors at Charlottetown in 1965, sending me a copy. The paper differed somewhat from the version later printed, since the original had a concluding hand-written section where Trudeau set out what he thought would be a "functional" approach to constitutional change. The first step, he argued, would involve "determining what values or benefits Canadians in general (this expression includes regional and cultural groups who deem themselves to be important) wish to see guaranteed as a right of every citizen throughout the whole extent of the territory: amongst other things, what degree of personal freedom, political liberty, economic security, cultural equality."[4] Appropriately, these fertile seeds of the Canadian Charter of Rights and Freedoms were planted at Charlottetown. Gestation took fourteen difficult years.

Premier Johnson of Quebec rejected Trudeau's charter proposal in an ad hominem attack on the minister of justice. Trudeau responded in kind and with a firmness that Ottawa had not had the courage to display in nearly a decade. The reviews of this solo performance were mostly positive, except in the Quebec nationalist press. I don't know what this moment meant in Trudeau's thinking about the leadership, but it certainly won him a bountiful harvest of potential supporters, and it energized those Liberals and others who were pressing him to accept the challenge.

ONE EVENING AT THE ROYAL YORK

Once the conference was over, Trudeau remained uncommitted publicly, but several of his colleagues, including Donald Macdonald and Jean Marchand (who believed that his own English was not sufficiently fluent to make him a credible candidate), were insistently urging him to join the race. Trudeau's interest was sufficient to tempt him to test the waters at the annual meeting of the Ontario Liberal Party in Toronto on 9 February. Forewarned of his presence by Ethel Teitelbaum, I went to the Royal York Hotel to watch. The scene was an extraordinary one, the first performance of the show that would soon be called Trudeaumania. While the declared leadership candidates moved through the friendly crowd, the delegates spontaneously swarmed the undeclared candidate. It seemed that everyone wanted an introduction, and many, apparently, urged him to run. Even more unexpected, at least for me, was his reaction. Obviously interested in his conversation with each well-wisher, Trudeau showed a certain shyness but no impatience or professorial cleverness. (Whenever he was later charged with arrogance, I recalled this and similar scenes when he displayed such ease with people who were genuinely interested in saying something to him. His arrogance, if that is what it was, was saved for those whose questions and comments arose not from an interest in his answers but from a desire to score points.)

I joined the throng of handshakers, and Trudeau asked if we could meet later. That evening we talked for about an hour and a half in Donald Macdonald's hotel suite. (Ruth Macdonald later told me that the discussion took place over a table decorated with her wig and that she waited nervously in an adjoining room until our discussion finished before reclaiming it.) Present were Trudeau and three others who were then strangers to me but were obviously part of the group that wanted to organize his leadership campaign – if only he could be convinced to let his name stand. These were Jean-Pierre Goyer, a young Quebec MP, who as a student had slept on the steps of the Quebec legislature to protest Duplessis's refusal to assist students financially; Jim Davey, a Montreal research scientist, who had been involved in Lesage's Liberal Party in 1960 but had grown disenchanted by its nationalist stance; and Gordon Gibson, a young motorcycle-riding British Columbia business-man. Don Macdonald was there, but perhaps only part of the time. He may have been organizing others who wanted to meet Trudeau after my departure. Here are my notes of the meeting, composed on 10 February 1968, when my historian's instinct told me that I had probably been present at an event that might lead to an even more important one. I have correct-ed spelling and typing errors:

Pierre seemed surprised and even a little confused by the extraordinary reception he had received in Toronto. It had obviously made his decision more difficult in the sense that he now realized that his decision would affect more people than he had realized.

He began the conversation by saying to the group that this had been a very striking demonstration of support, though its real meaning was still to be assessed. Then he pulled his legs up on the sofa, pressed his hands on his skull, pulled his hair forward over his forehead and turned to me and said: "What do you make of this whole thing Ramsay? You're an outsider, a disinterested observer even though you have always said friendly things about me. Tell me what you think it means as an historian. You know Quebec as an out-sider, and though we usually agree about the meaning of things in Quebec, your judgment is better than mine, because I am involved on the inside and am, to some extent, maybe a hostile observer. Will they call me *un roi nègre*, will I fall under the same criticisms as Laurier and will I get the Uncle Louis image?

I said that, of course, some people will call him a *vendu* – just as they'd said of Laurier and St. Laurent; that was inevitable. But did that really represent the thinking of Quebecers? After all, they'd voted for Laurier and Uncle Louis regardless of what the nationalist intellectuals had said. Moreover I said that it was a great chance to make French Canadians look to the federal government again, to identify in a personal way. Mercier had turned French Canadians in upon Quebec, but Laurier's election in 1896 had changed it all again. Maybe you could do the same.

Jim said he fully agreed – said he had worked with Sauvé from '59 through the 1960 provincial election and had found that nationalism was not an important factor when people voted.

Pierre seemed very interested in the comment about Laurier and asked me to repeat it. But then he wondered if Sauvé's argument that it was the wrong time for a French Canadian wasn't accurate. Said he and the others had come to Ottawa to get a job done, and had believed that winning the prime ministership was unimportant as long as they had someone who was open, and could be convinced that certain things had to be done. Pearson had fulfilled that function nearly perfectly. Wouldn't an English Canadian be better as an interlocutor with the English Canadian provinces?

I said it depended on two things. Was there such an English Canadian available? And secondly, now that linguistic questions had been nearly settled, was it really a question of moving the English Canadian provinces on specifically French Canadian things, or had the whole thing now not become rather one of federal-provincial relations, and if so, wasn't Sauvé's argument passé? Pierre said that was probably so.

Goyer said that the point really was that Pierre obviously didn't think there was a suitable English Canadian alterna-

tive, or he wouldn't even be considering the leadership.
Pierre demurred somewhat, but not totally.

He then turned to the matter of experience – he had so little real understanding of how the overall government process worked. I told him he had as much or more cabinet experience as Laurier, about the same amount as King, and only a little less than St. Laurent – and a great deal more than Diefenbaker. Again he showed great interest in the comment on Laurier. I added that some of the candidates had too much experience – they were too set in their ways – this was obviously the case with Martin. Pierre interjected that if Martin won, at least they would get someone in External!

I asked him how he would fare in a campaign when asked about matters other than those he had been dealing with since joining the cabinet – economic policy, agriculture, Vietnam.

He said his responses would be platitudes. He was only now getting to the place where he could run the Department of Justice with 12 hours a day of work, and he had no time to think of other issues. Referred to the Watkins Report saying it had been available for ten days, he had not read it, and would not be able to for three months. This was a serious problem – he was too much of a specialist.

I asked him if he was interested in the range of government policies. He said, definitely yes. His major frustration was that he got so involved in the constitution – he had wanted to come into the Cabinet without portfolio so he could have a chance to learn, but this had not worked out. He was deeply interested in economic policy and especially foreign policy – he would have liked to have been Minister of External Affairs, but all that had passed by because of the constitution.

I responded by saying that I could understand his frustration, but that his whole career had shown that he was a "generalist," that with help he could quickly learn the necessary to conduct discussions of all areas of policy, because his background was so broad.

At this point someone said, do you really want this job, do you feel you could do it? Pierre responded without hesitation that he would like the job in the abstract, and that if he had enough experience he would feel that he could do it. But the point was he was afraid that he could not meet his own standards of excellence, he wasn't sure he was ready.

Jim said that this was a judgment that had to come partly as a result of collective judgment – obviously there were many people who thought he was ready, that he could do the job.

Pierre replied saying that though Jim's arguments were usually convincing, this one was not. This was the kind of decision that required that he be satisfied by his own criterion – that the popular judgment was unsound in these matters, that his gut and his brain had to agree. It was a philosophical question – was his destiny determined by outside forces or by inner direction. He had always disciplined himself to be inner directed. He had always worked alone – there were always chances to take up new jobs that were pressed on him from outside, but that he had always told himself to stick to what he was doing no matter what the outside pressures. There might be other chances to be party leader, when he was more prepared.

I asked him about the personal sacrifice involved. He said he didn't care. He had made that decision when he went into politics – to be p.m. wouldn't make that much difference – he might have to take his holidays differently, that was all.

For the rest the decision had been taken, so he might as well be first man as second.

We returned to the question of whether this was the best way of getting the job done that he and his friends had come to Ottawa to do. I said that the job could only be done if good men stayed in Ottawa – Marc Lalonde, Jean Beetz and so on. That meant that they had to have a prime minister that they could work with. Moreover if the job was to continue, then the Liberals had to win an election and all signs seemed to indicate that Stanfield was a fairly good bet against the already declared candidates. Pierre agreed with the first part; he was more diffident about his ability to win an election.

Then he said what he needed was rest, followed by 24 hours of solitude, to make up his mind – it was too easy to say yes when he was tired. About this time, three Winnipeg lawyers – John Lamonte, Scott Wright and Joe O'Sullivan – arrived, and I left.

My general impression from as disinterested a view as I can take, was that I was talking to a genuinely undecided man. His honesty, and his modesty, were the two overwhelming characteristics that struck me. He knows his strengths and his weaknesses, he is above all his "own man" and will decide on the basis of his own assessment of his own ability to fulfill the job – by which he means to continue the evolution of Canadian federalism, lead the party, win an election, and be at peace with himself. There is no doubt about his commitment to politics as the way of getting what is right, in his view, done.[5]

The evening had been an extraordinary, almost unbelievable, one. My previous direct contacts with politics and politicians was minimal. I had talked at length with M.J. Coldwell, the CCF leader, while researching my MA thesis – he had impressed me deeply – and later occasionally had met with David Lewis through my friend and colleague Ken McNaught. I had been a delegate to the NDP's founding convention and had made a few speeches to "New Party" groups. Speaking to a union meeting in the autumn of 1961, for instance, I had asserted that the Quebec Liberals would never nationalize hydro. (Early the following week, Premier Lesage announced the decision to nationalize, adopting the slogan, *Maîtres chez nous* – and Gord Brigden, the party secretary, called to ask if I had any further predictions.) Once or twice, together with York professor Ed Broadbent, I had met with Donald MacDonald, the Ontario leader of the NDP, to discuss policy ideas. But active politics had never attracted me. I preferred teaching, research, and writing, including comment on politics and politicians. Trudeau had never struck me as a potential politician, of course. His interest in politics seemed to stop where mine did, though I was vaguely aware of his unsuccessful attempts in the 1950s to organize anti-Duplessis movements. But now he had jumped into active politics and had sought my advice about entering the Liberal Party leadership contest. Pretty heady stuff for an associate professor!

The discussion that night at the Royal York, with its historical and philosophical dimensions, was much like all the discussions we had had in the past. The fact that we still didn't belong to the same political party didn't seem to matter. After all, we were friends. Donald Macdonald later described our Toronto conversation this way: "There was this strange way this guy could go into a huge crowd and be pushed and pulled everywhere, and then minutes later, in that quiet little room upstairs he would be talking with Ramsay Cook as if he had

An undecided Pierre Trudeau leaves a room in the Royal York Hotel,
10 February 1968

been reading in a library all day. I think I noticed it first in Toronto. And I knew then that there was no danger of the adulation reaching him."[6]

Trudeau had several other discussions after I left the Royal York. Later that night a photographer caught him leaving Macdonald's room as he paused, either in thought or exhaustion, to pull on his gloves. His dark hair, sparse on the top, broad forehead, high cheekbones, and especially his downcast eyes were all composed in a way that suggested indecision. The delegations that had followed me, I decided when I saw the photo the next day, had not done any better than I had. It is my favourite photo of Pierre.

PIERRE FOR PRIME MINISTER

Late the next afternoon, 11 February, Jim Davey called to say that he had taken Trudeau to the airport the previous evening and that the noncandidate had been struck by my argument about Laurier's and King's inexperience. Trudeau, he said, was closer to a decision to run than he had been in "numerous" previous discussions. These arguments would now be used to counteract those who, like Claude Ryan, were trying to throw cold water on the Trudeau boom. But the decision was still to come, for Trudeau had set out five conditions:

1 There had to be evidence of party machinery that would ensure that his candidacy would not end in disaster. Davey said Claude Frenette, president of the Quebec federal Liberal organization, would ensure this.

2 Said his friends must give some assurance that they would not desert him – by this he meant the friends whom he

had taken to Ottawa. Davey said Lalonde had given this assurance.

3 His personal qualifications – he still had to be certain in his own mind that he was satisfied with his own abilities to meet the standards he would set for himself in the job.

4 Senior civil servants – he had to be sure that the Ottawa bureaucracy would work with him. He implied that this might mean some changes at the top in the civil service.

5 There was the matter of his cabinet colleagues – would they accept him if they [sic] won, and would some of them be willing to support his candidacy? This was to be looked into this week.[7]

It was obvious from this conversation with Davey that many wheels had already been put in motion. Particularly important was the role of the Quebec young Liberals – Claude Frenette was one of them – in pushing for a Trudeau candidacy. Davey had gone on to say that his own job now was to fly senior Liberals from across the country to Ottawa to speak with Trudeau. Obviously, these introductions were necessary to start a national campaign. If the consultations were a success and made Trudeau comfortable about winning solid support, and if his own reflections convinced him of his ability to do the job, then Jean Marchand would tell the Quebec caucus on Wednesday that he would not run and that Pierre Trudeau was their man. Once the constitutional debate in the House was held, Trudeau would announce his candidacy.

Marc Lalonde told me in June 1968 that the campaign to convince Trudeau to run had begun while Trudeau was on holiday in Tahiti over Christmas. He remembered that Pearson and Marchand had sent a telegram to Trudeau begging him not to speak to the press on his return from vacation, since they feared that he would say *jamais* if asked about the leadership. He went on to say that Trudeau had remained genuinely undecided, despite constant pressure from leading ministers and MPs. Both Lalonde and Michael Pitfield had gone over the ground with him several times. Only after the famous late-night walk in the snow in his long fur coat did he make his decision. Even then he changed it the next day when he discovered division in the Quebec caucus. Although Lalonde didn't say so, Maurice Sauvé was obviously the problem; he eventually supported Paul Martin. When Trudeau met the press on Friday, 16 February, only he knew what he would say.

He accepted the challenge. That same Friday, Eleanor and I wired him our congratulations and good wishes, signing the telegram "Two Innocents in the Liberal Party," though neither of us was a member of the party. (Eleanor never did become one, but I soon joined the St Paul's Liberal Riding Association, along with quite few other new Liberals: I wanted to ensure that the delegates to the convention supported Trudeau rather than Ian Wahn's choice, Paul Hellyer. We succeeded.) The following Monday, Tom Ford, a public relations person charged with preparing a Trudeau press kit, called. He asked that I write a statement designed to meet arguments about Trudeau's inexperience and also a summary of his constitutional principles. I agreed and noted laconically, "The campaign is moving, it would seem."[8]

Joining the Liberal Party, even if only temporarily, meant my resignation from the NDP. It was not an easy decision, as I explained in my letter to John Harney, the provincial secretary, on 25 February: "It has taken me a long time to reach this decision, but Mr. MacDonald's [leader of the Ontario

NDP] remarks on the recent Constitutional Conference indicated that my views on this subject and those of the party are completely incompatible. I am very sorry about this for I think that most of the other objectives of the NDP are entirely worthy of support. But at this moment there is nothing more fundamental in my mind than the constitutional issue and here, rightly or wrongly, I find myself out-of-line with NDP policy and in total agreement with the federal Liberal party. For this reason I have reluctantly decided to leave the NDP." Harney replied in a friendly manner, recognizing my "honest, explicit and sincere" differences with the party. My resignation, he continued, would save "us the difficulty and embarrassment of asking you just what your intentions were toward Mr. Trudeau."[9] He refunded my membership fees. No other party would have done that! He also expressed his profound disagreement with Trudeau's constitutional position, describing it as a threat to the country. (About a decade later, John Harney became Jean-Paul Harney and headed into oblivion as leader of the Quebec provincial NDP on a quasi-separatist platform.)

Shortly after Trudeau declared his candidacy, the CBC asked me to interview two of his parliamentary critics, Davie Fulton, a former Conservative minister of justice, and David Lewis, the NDP constitutional spokesman. They thoroughly agreed that Trudeau was too "rigid" in his attitude to Quebec, though neither objected to the proposed charter of rights. Each in turn attacked the government and the minister of justice for refusing to establish a parliamentary committee on the constitution so that all parties and the public could participate in the process of constitutional change. I then asked each of these politicians if their parties had specific constitutional proposals to make to such a committee. Each answered in the affirmative. After the program, David Lewis, whom I had known and admired for about a decade, drew me aside and invited me to join an NDP committee to work out a constitutional position. I declined, but before recovering from my surprise at this apparent admission that his party did not have a position, Davie Fulton pressed me to join a similar committee that his party was about to organize. My continuing doubts about my new allegiance to the Liberal Party, or at least to its minister of justice, almost vanished after these amazing encounters.

The following day I met briefly with Trudeau in his West Block office and discovered how comfortable he was with his decision to contest the leadership, though he was certainly not overly optimistic about his chances. He remarked that campaigning while the House was sitting was practically impossible, since the minority government was at constant risk. Pearson had ordered the candidates not to jeopardize the government by campaigning, a warning that Trudeau (though not all of his fellow candidates) took seriously. In fact, at one point the government had actually been defeated and had stayed in power only through a skilful manoeuvre. As I sat in the gallery during Question Period that afternoon, I was impressed by my friend's growing parliamentary skills. If he could win the leadership, I thought, he could lead the party and defend a government. But could he win? I waited and watched.

THE CAMPAIGN

I played no direct role in Trudeau's campaign for the leadership. This was often frustrating, for I was extremely anxious that he should win. Still, I had not really left the NDP, at least mentally, and I never did become comfortable with most Liberals, apart from my French Canadian friends and a few others, such as Ethel Teitelbaum. Nor was I overly impressed with Trudeau's campaign strategy which, for all that the crowds gathered to see and hear him, seemed disorganized. Of course, I knew nothing about political organization, and there was something appealing about the apparent amateurism of my friend's entourage. But I worried that his great opportunity might be lost through mismanagement.

The worry and frustration intensified during an apparently triumphant appearance at the St Lawrence Hall in Toronto on 3 March. Pierre still didn't perform like a politician. His speech was bland and general. But in the question period he was scintillatingly brilliant. Typical was his response to a journalist – George Bain, I think – who asked him what he would think of a leadership candidate from Ontario who was opposed by the premier of the province, the major church leaders, and the most influential newspapers. "I'd think he had a lot of guts," Trudeau shot back – to the delight of the audience, who recognized, of course, that the questioner was referring to Trudeau's Quebec reputation. Still, the evening left me very uneasy, especially a "seminar" later that evening at Bill Kilbourn's house in Rosedale, where Trudeau met with a group of Toronto intellectuals.

The next day I wrote to Marc Lalonde, who at this stage was still working for Prime Minister Pearson and therefore was seemingly neutral in the leadership campaign. I did not want, I said, to bother Pierre, "who has so many things on his mind," and I added, "I also don't want to appear to intrude on him, or to leave the impression that I have any right to be offering advice on his campaign. I hope you don't mind me writing to you this way," I told Lalonde, "but I am sure that you will understand that I have no personal axe to grind, and my sole interest is in seeing Pierre succeed." I had, I think, convinced myself that Pierre Trudeau's constitutional reform ideas and his ability to restore the confidence of French Canadians in the federal system was my sole reason for taking up his cause. Neither then nor later had I any ambition beyond that, though the idea that a personal friend might become prime minister of Canada did have a certain appeal.

In this letter, I first gave Lalonde my impression of the town hall meeting: "Pierre's public appearance here was a very great success. He has a tremendous capacity to communicate with audiences, much more than I would ever have expected. His speaking style is superb, and his sense of occasion and timing nearly perfect. My own impression was that his speech was rather general in some places, but of course his time was so limited that it was impossible to get much beyond the general. And I also know that there is the problem of cabinet solidarity. His performance in the question period was absolutely first-class. His wit and charm and also the seriousness with which he treated every question was most impressive."

I then turned to what I thought was the less successful side of the Toronto visit. Several of my media friends had complained bitterly about Trudeau's staff, none of whom were known to me. The staff, the complaint went, simply got in the way, sometimes seeming more interested in displaying their relationship with Trudeau than in ensuring his exposure to the press and TV representatives. While I could not assess the validity of these complaints, some came from friendly sources. "I have had a long conversation with Don Newlands of the *Star Weekly*," I told Lalonde. "As you know he is a photographer and an old friend of Pierre's. He said that many press people were annoyed with the weekend's events and that this could backfire against Pierre. He said relations with the press were handled very badly and that the source of the problem was that Merle Shane and a man named Porteous, who is apparently press liaison officer, seemed really incompetent."

Newlands had also wondered whether Trudeau was really meeting voting delegates at these big rallies or whether he was just attracting a curious public. As it turned out, though I didn't understand it at the time, Trudeau's strategy was to appeal to the voters generally, believing that if he could demonstrate his ability to win an election, then the delegates would come to him. Moreover, his own critical attitude to journalists convinced him that speaking directly to the public was his most effective weapon. Still, I was not entirely wrong that the campaign organization needed a good deal of fine-tuning.

What bothered me most about Trudeau's foray into Toronto was the private meeting at Bill Kilbourn's house. I don't know who initiated it or how the participants were chosen, but it was obviously based on the belief that the candidate needed a brains trust, especially in matters of foreign policy. This is what I told Lalonde about this session, one in which I took part but said very little:

The second matter is far more important, and I expect Pierre is aware of it. After the meeting I attended a "policy discussion" with Pierre, a couple of his aides and some people who had been gathered together by Bill Kilbourn. In my judgment it was a terrible waste of Pierre's time; for all he got out of it he would have been better off getting some rest. The problem was two-fold. First of all the people who were to give Pierre some ideas on foreign policy were people without any ideas chiefly because they are former civil service establishment people whose usefulness was once very great, but who are now exhausted volcanoes. Pierre's instincts in foreign policy are to look for new directions – his public statements on Friday night were refreshingly frank and undogmatic. In this field I think Pierre's best bet is to try and define general goals. The people he talked to after the meeting take Canadian foreign policy, which they helped to make long ago, as forever settled. They would be good advisors for Robert Winters but not for Pierre whose greatest asset is his obvious desire to break with all the clichés of the past. The second thing was that these people, because they accept as given the principles of Canadian foreign policy, talked to Pierre only about details. I could see from what he was saying that his desire was to develop a general approach and in this he found no help. I had the feeling that Jim Davey shared my frustrations in this conversation – and I think probably Pierre did too. Since his time is so short I hate to see it wasted this way. He can get all the technical advice that he needs after he becomes Prime Minister. At this point he needs to be encouraged to follow his own instinct to think out loud, and in fairly general ways, about Canadian foreign policy.[10]

Since I knew, as no doubt did the invited experts, whose names I did not record (though I recall the presence of John Holmes, earlier a distinguished foreign service officer and in 1968 president of the CIIA), that Pierre was strongly anti-nuclear, I thought of him as somewhat radical in foreign policy matters. Or so I hoped. Personally, he probably favoured withdrawal from NATO and greater Canadian emphasis on the Third World. So I had little time for the establishment line that was fed to Trudeau that night in Bill Kilbourn's study. (The "ladies," our wives, had been left in the living room, doubtless so that they could discuss matters more suited to them.)

I did not speak to Pierre about the policy discussion afterwards, but it had no noticeable impact on him. He earned, in the Department of External Affairs, a deserved reputation for mistrusting bureaucratic advice. After all, he once observed that he could learn as much from reading the *New York Times* as he could from External's memos! Geoff Pearson, who never liked Trudeau, once told me that I was thought to be Trudeau's adviser on foreign policy. That would certainly have put the national interest in jeopardy, though it is true that I helped to write a major speech on foreign policy for him during the 1968 election. Then Ivan Head took over.

Whether my advice was sound or not on this occasion, it was apparently welcome. Lalonde let me know that Jim Davey entirely agreed with my comments and had already taken steps to "keep matters under control and correct the deficiencies" that I had noticed.[11] Viewed from afar at least, Trudeau's campaign continued along what seemed to be its often chaotic course, but I played no further role in it. I had another month of teaching, and I was already beginning to think about taking up a visiting professorship at Harvard the coming autumn. This was also my last term at the University of Toronto, for I had decided to move north to the cold wind-swept York University campus. Leaving the University of Toronto and the NDP in the same year obviously suggested some psychological instability, a mid-life crisis at thirty-six!

Early in March, the English version of Trudeau's *Federalism and the French Canadians* appeared, now almost guaranteed bestseller status. Bill French, the book editor of the *Globe and Mail*, asked me to write a review. He didn't ask if I had a conflict of interest, but I suggested to him that I did. Even so, he still wanted me to do it, so I agreed, on condition that I could combine the review of Trudeau's book with a forthcoming translation of René Lévesque's *Option Québec,* the French edition of which had already sold about 80,000 copies. He agreed, and on 14 March the review appeared under the title "Populizer versus Thinker." Lovely black-and-white drawings of the impressive heads of these two young politicians graced the top of the page. I had tried to be even-handed, though my preference for Trudeau's rational analysis over Lévesque's oratorical flourishes was obvious. The conclusion expressed my sense of the drama that these leaders symbolized: "The battle of the books has now set forth, with greater or lesser clarity, their visions of the best future for French Canadians. Each wants greater equality and a better way of life for his compatriots, but their roads to these goals are totally at variance. That this is so is perhaps the central tragedy of contemporary Canada."[12]

The review had some impact. About a week after it appeared, Lévesque made it the subject of a vigorous denunciation in a speech he gave at St Michael's College. As I entered the hall late, Father Kelly, the intelligent and droll college president, told me how pleased he was that I had provoked Lévesque into making such a rousing speech. Two weeks later, one of Trudeau's nominators quoted my review at length as a reason to make him leader of the Liberal Party. I guess I had not been quite as even-handed as I had thought. On top of this, the *Globe* paid me fifty dollars, so I have always thought of that piece of writing as bringing me both fame and fortune.

Lectures completed, I headed for Ottawa on 3 April to watch the Liberal Convention, having arranged to stay with Blair and Jacqueline Neatby. On Friday, Blair and I wandered around the Coliseum, dropping in at various "bear-pit" sessions. John Turner (my least favourite candidate), speaking at a session on constitutional matters, seemed to go out of his way to differentiate himself from Trudeau, arguing that the minister of justice was too rigid in his approach to Quebec. Later, when Blair and I visited Trudeau in his campaign trailer and I reported the remark to him, he replied, obviously irritated, "He said that, did he?" But almost nothing else was said about the campaign. Instead, Trudeau introduced us to Jean Martineau, one of the radical young Liberals who had founded the Action libérale nationale in 1934. He had been chosen to move Trudeau's nomination that night. Trudeau told Martineau that Neatby and I were historians who might be interested in hearing his views about Quebec politics in the 1930s. And so, for nearly half an hour, the four of us talked about Martineau, Paul Gouin, Maurice Duplessis, and others. (Martineau had never been co-opted into the Union Nationale.) Trudeau seemed more interested in this past history than in anything happening on the convention floor – that is to say, his future. He had again reverted to his favourite persona of intellectual. Wishing him well, we departed, somewhat disappointed in our failure to elicit any campaign gossip. That, and not a history lesson, is what we historians had come for! Afterwards I realized that this had been another demonstration of Trudeau's greatest strength and the characteristic for which I most admired him – his self-discipline. No one's man but his own.

That same night I attended the candidate's speeches and demonstrations. After the hospitality suites and the thumping, raucous disco dancing at the Chaudière Club the previous night, this was pretty tame stuff. What appeared to be the spontaneous eruption of Trudeau signs as he entered the Coliseum alone excited everyone, including me. Trudeau's speech was flat, but few seemed to notice, the medium having become the message. Since I was now identified with Trudeau, several journalists questioned me about my role. Val Sears of the *Toronto*

Star, a likable and able NDP-inclined reporter, asked me about the petition I had circulated. Bill Kilbourn was his source. So I told him a few details, which either he or I made sound much more important than they were. This became part of the story of the rise of Pierre Trudeau that would be regularly repeated by journalists and scholars, most of whom failed to realize that it was really Jean Marchand, Marc Lalonde, and the Quebec wing of the Liberal Party that had given Trudeau his chance.

I never saw Trudeau again that weekend, even to congratulate him. Not being a delegate, I had no vote. I spent the emotional evening of the great victory with the Neatbys at the home of Charles and Monique Lussier, friends of Trudeau from *Cité libre* days. The others present were all civil servants and all French Canadians, each with some earlier association with the man who was about to become prime minister. When the final ballot was announced, I cried with joy, Jacqueline Neatby claims. I don't remember it, but it is certainly possible, even probable. As I had written to Marc Lalonde a month earlier, "Pierre's chances of winning are now very great, and I want so much to see him win." The "disinterested observer" of February, like hundreds of thousands of other Canadians, had lost his detachment, lost it to a chance acquaintance who had become a friend. Now the friend would be prime minister.

On Sunday I returned to Eleanor and the kids in Toronto, exhausted, exhilarated, and anxious. I had only once voted for a leader (Tommy Douglas) and never for a candidate who had been a winner in any election. That made voting easier and ensured my independence as a scholar and political commentator. Being on the losing side ensured that I was always right. As Adlai Stevenson had once paraphrased one of my favourite historians, "Absolute power corrupts, lack of power corrupts absolutely." Now I was on the winning side and more. Having urged Pierre to fight for the leadership, I could not now withdraw into detachment and return to the opposition. Not that he had extracted any promises from me. On the contrary, he had always urged me back to my books, the important work. But it was not in my nature to turn my back on my friend, especially since he seemed to me the best hope we had to prevent the fragmentation of the country. He was not rigid in his constitutional views, he was just clear. That is what convinced me to separate myself politically from some of my oldest and closest teachers and friends. They were real friends, as events proved, for our differences were only political. My longtime friend Kay Sigurjonsson frequently and sternly left me in no doubt about her disapproval. Ken McNaught shared most of my views of Trudeau, but never voted for him. Jean Crowe presented me with a 1923 autographed photo of Mackenzie King, the unkindest cut of all! Anyway, I had come home after Pierre's triumph, stage one. Now I could sit back and watch events unfold, leaving him in the competent hands that had helped him take charge of the Liberal Party and the Government of Canada. Or so I thought.

INTO THE 1968 ELECTION

The new prime minister, as I had reason to expect, lost no time in calling an election in order to capitalize on the enthusiasm that his leadership campaign had aroused. He had become well known, in a superficial fashion, across the country. But he had also raised immense expectations, all of them rather vague. Before the realization set in that he was neither a magician nor even the bearer of an elixir to ensure a permanent spirit of

Expo '67, he wanted to replace the Pearson minority by a Trudeau majority. My plan, as far as I had one that went beyond grading essays and examination papers, was to watch it happen. Convinced that a weak minority government would relapse into the vacillating policies of the Pearson years – policies that I feared would eventually be destructive of the federal system – I shared Trudeau's hope for a majority government, one with strong support in Quebec and with representation in every region. Voting Liberal for Ian Wahn would be an entirely new experience for me, one that not even Trudeau's leadership made entirely pleasurable.

Sitting back watching it happen proved impossible. To begin with, I found a Liberal candidate who appealed to me more than my own sitting member. My alderman, Charles Caccia, decided to contest the nomination in Walter Gordon's former riding of Davenport. While I was not acquainted with Caccia, I knew that he had an excellent reputation for progressive views and hard work in city politics. My interest in the Davenport outcome had also been sparked by a call late in April from Stephen Clarkson, then a young political scientist at the University of Toronto. I knew him slightly, since we had both been members of the University League for Social Reform. During the few years of its existence, it had brought together left-leaning academics to discuss Canadian problems and possible solutions. (We were better at problems than at solutions.) I had also met his wife Adrienne socially and seen her on television. Stephen asked me over for a drink, and soon after my arrival I realized that it was my Trudeau connection that explained the invitation. I don't remember the order, but I received two requests. Adrienne wondered if I could help her convince the new prime minister to appear on her television program. Stephen wondered if I could arrange a personal meeting with

Trudeau as a step towards becoming a candidate for the Liberal nomination in Davenport.

Both requests surprised me. First, perhaps naively, I had never thought of myself in this new role as dispenser of Trudeau-related favours. Secondly, Stephen Clarkson's political ambition came as a total surprise. When I asked him about this, he replied that he had spent a term at Columbia during the early stages of the Robert Kennedy campaign and he had been politicized. Moreover, he felt that his personal relationship to Walter Gordon gave him a claim on the seat even though he lived in Rosedale, as had Gordon. I wished him well, in fact I wished both of them well, but explained that I had no special influence with Pierre Trudeau in such matters. Politics, I had begun to realize, was not entirely about ideas. Shortly after Trudeau's leadership victory, I had run into Cranford Pratt, a distinguished professor of African affairs. He congratulated me on my role in Trudeau's success and remarked, half seriously I think, that he expected me to become the Canadian representative at the Court of St James. I was actually hoping for Hanoi or the Vatican.

Clarkson decided to take the plunge even without the hoped-for imprimatur. As a popular young professor, he signed up a large number of student delegates. The nominating meeting on 9 May swelled to such a size that it had to be held in the Coliseum at the CNE grounds. There were said to be ten thousand delegates looking at four contenders. I tagged along with my friend Jack Saywell, who was freelancing for the CBC. Stephen and Adrienne Clarkson were installed in a box, and when the floodlights passed over them, Adrienne, in a sequined dress, glittered beside her hopeful husband. After each interminable vote, Saywell and I headed out to a local bar for a drink and to poll the delegates who joined us. As the night wore on,

Clarkson's chances dwindled as his student supporters slipped away to cram for final exams, or to sleep. At 2:30 AM, after seven hours of voting and counting, Caccia emerged the winner. Many of his main opponent's working-class supporters, who had jobs to do the next day, had gone home. I was very pleased, but also stunned by the enthusiasm that Trudeau's leadership had obviously aroused. I later realized that the Davenport nominating meeting had attracted more people than any event that Robert Stanfield addressed during the entire spring campaign. Trudeau met bigger crowds – nearly fifty thousand in Nathan Phillips Square late in the campaign – but this was just a nominating meeting.

"AND YOU DIDN'T WRITE IT!"

Shortly after Charles Caccia's triumph, I was drawn directly into the election battle, not on home ground but in Ottawa. On 10 May Marc Lalonde invited me to work in Trudeau's office for a few weeks. I agreed, with a sense of both excitement and apprehension. The excitement was in anticipation of seeing the campaign from the inside when working with Lalonde and Trudeau. The apprehension came from the realization that the break with my political past would now be complete. On the following Tuesday I moved into a small room in a Chateau Laurier Hotel turret overlooking Parliament Hill. My job would be speech writing and the preparation of information on a variety of subjects about which the prime minister might need briefing. My special assignment was the constitution, watching for Robert Stanfield and Marcel Faribault or Tommy Douglas and Robert Cliche to contradict each other. The wait was not long.

Lalonde was at the centre of the prime minister's staff, which was quite small. Most of its members travelled on the election tour with the prime minister: Jim Davey, Gordon Gibson, Roméo LeBlanc, Tim Porteous, Pierre Levasseur, and Bill Lee, one of the few experienced campaigners who had come over from Paul Hellyer's office. On the campaign tour, local organizers often joined this group. In Ottawa, Lalonde ran the government almost alone, though he was in regular touch with Michael Pitfield, clerk of the Privy Council, and with various other officials, as well as with cabinet ministers when they were not campaigning. On one occasion, even I helped Lalonde run the country. Together we decided to lower the flag to half mast to mark Robert Kennedy's assassination – against the advice of the protocol office at External Affairs.

Michel Vennat and I worked in the Prime Minister's Office with Lalonde. Over at Liberal Headquarters, another group slaved away under the direction of Senator John Nichol, the party president, but I had almost no contact with them. Mostly I worked in my room at the Chateau Laurier or in the East Block with Lalonde, sometimes sitting at the prime minister's desk. This unleashed no uncontrollable ambitions. Occasionally I answered letters for the prime minister, for they arrived by the boxcar. In my replies I often chided correspondents who had silly complaints, causing Lalonde to decide that the job was best left to Mary Macdonald. She had been Pearson's loyal secretary and had diplomatic experience. "You're too like Pierre," laughed Lalonde.

That was probably why I was asked to write speeches: I knew what Trudeau thought. There was another reason too. On the tour, Tim Porteous prepared material for Trudeau, but because of the pressures of each day and the leader's preference for improvisation, reports of style often took precedence over substance. Lalonde explained to me at the outset that Trudeau had to differentiate himself from the other parties in both content and approach – clearly but not radically. In my diary I noted, "Marc made the point that while the party obviously intended to capitalize on Pierre's personality, it would not be satisfactory either to the party or Pierre to have a campaign which was merely a competition of images." This view reassured me, because in these early days of the campaign the substance of the prime minister's speeches was thin, and since I was still being an NDPer at heart, this left me very unhappy.

I soon realized that there was another problem. Measured by the crowds he drew, Trudeau's campaign seemed to be going famously. But what did the crowds mean? He was certainly puzzled. Returning one night from a rally in Winnipeg with several bushels of wilted flowers, children's toys, and other miscellaneous mementos, he quizzed us repeatedly: What was this all about? Was anyone listening to what he said in his speeches? (which typically were delivered from truck flatbeds in supermarket plazas. "Plaza Pierre," his opponents called him enviously.) He was genuinely concerned, though as the caterpillar gradually metamorphosed into a politician, he was pleased that he could draw huge crowds. The problem, however, was that the press was left without texts and wrote endlessly about Trudeaumania, rarely even mentioning the content of his off-the-cuff talks. Obviously, if the message was not being reported, maybe not even delivered, the time had come for more formal, written presentations than his overworked assistants on the plane could produce. This described my assignment.

To help me prepare the first speech, devoted to "national unity," Lalonde gave me various confidential documents, the most important being the briefing papers for the constitutional conference of the previous February. This document of several hundred pages, of which Lalonde was justly proud, set out the federal constitutional position. It combined Trudeau's basic position with a strategy designed to defend the federal government against Quebec's claims to primacy in the protection and development of French Canadian rights in Canada. At the heart of the strategy was a proposed "Sequence of Constitutional Discussions," whose aim was to focus the talks on a proposed charter of rights, including language rights, thus avoiding any early discussions of the division of powers, where Quebec might win allies in other provinces. Although I did not fully recognize it at the time, this paper set out the essentials of the position that Trudeau would doggedly adhere to until he finally reached his goal in 1981. Reading this document, I was again struck by the similarity of my own views with those of Trudeau and Lalonde. I had outlined a similar strategy in a recent *Forum* piece.

The national unity speech, entitled "The Just Society," was completed on 15 May, in time for a major appearance in Montreal. Trudeau read it, graded it, as was his professorial habit, delivered his refined version, and released mine to the press. Today it reads more like the professor who wrote it than the ex-professor who delivered it in his own style.[13] Nevertheless it was a triumph. *Le Devoir*, for example, which had done its best to ignore Trudeau's campaign speeches so far, published my speech in full. Other newspapers reported it fully and even used large excerpts, doubtless needing filler. This was exactly what we wanted, and it was a confirmation of my suspicion that a reporter without a text is a reporter without a story. Lalonde then asked me to stay on as long as I could to pull together more texts for Trudeau to pass out, even if they remained undelivered. It seemed a good combination and was confirmed when Lalonde commissioned a very literate academic, Douglas LePan, to provide an urban policy text for a major Toronto appearance. Trudeau delivered it verbatim. It was an utter flop as a political speech, though the thousands gathered in Nathan Phillips Square didn't seem to mind how long he droned on abstractly about the wonders of the city through the ages. Next day the newspaper concentrated on Trudeaumania.

So the pattern was set. Speeches were written, delivered partly or not at all, but regularly handed out to the press, and almost as regularly reported as if delivered. For a Sudbury meeting on 5 June, I cobbled together an uninspiring statement on mining and natural resource policy – "Northern Problems and the Just Society." Neither the writer nor, I suspect, the designated speaker, knew much about the topic. It hardly mattered, for that very day Sirhan Sirhan assassinated Robert Kennedy. Trudeau arrived in Sudbury directly from André Laurendeau's funeral in Montreal, where he had been made to feel not entirely welcome by some of the nationalists present. The road from Sudbury airport to the city was lined by adoring fans. Abandoning my speech, Trudeau passionately improvised before a large attentive crowd. He spoke of his friend Laurendeau and of his own fundamental beliefs: tolerance, liberty, the need to accept cultural and linguistic diversity, and the threat that violence represented to peaceful democracies if justice was denied. Reported on national television, it was Trudeau the philosopher politician at his best.[14] Lalonde told me that after seeing the TV news reports, Lester Pearson had phoned to say that it was the finest political speech he had ever heard. At the Ottawa airport that night, where we went to meet the conquering hero, I complimented him on his brilliant speech. "Thanks," he said putting his arm on my shoulder and smiling wickedly, "And you didn't write it!"

While scribbling speeches dealing with most things under the sun, I was also given the job of assembling a briefing book for the party leaders' mid-campaign television debate. This would be the first in Canada – irresistible now that it had become a regular feature of presidential elections in the United States. Trudeau's advisers were not enthusiastic about the debate because, unlike the U.S. debate, in which two candidates received equal time, the Canadian version would allow each leader the same opportunity to speak: three to attack, one to defend. Moreover, Trudeau's popularity would ensure the other leaders an audience that they could not attract on their own. Nevertheless, everyone was confident that he would more than hold his own. A debate there would be. I did my best to help by compiling a fat summary of the other leaders' policy statements on major and minor questions, along with statistics on GNP, immigration, government expenditures, employment, grain prices, timber exports, and whatever else seemed useful. Trudeau went into the 9 June debate stuffed, and his performance reflected his bloated condition. Stiff and humourless, he regurgitated the material that he had obviously studied with his usual concentration. Robert Stanfield was not much better, handing the English debate to Tommy Douglas, an old stager who alone kept the viewing audience awake. Réal Caouette, effective even in English, triumphed in French. Trudeau, for the first time since he entered Parliament, was vanquished. I should have been fired.

Returning to Ottawa after this debacle, I joined a group of gloomy Trudeauites in the East Block. Jim Davey was especially down, but even Lalonde, who was usually ready with a smile and a shrug when things went poorly, was obviously upset. They considered launching an all-out assault on Tommy Douglas for what they considered his repeated misrepresentations of Trudeau's policy positions. John Nichol favoured this approach. I dissented. That would only draw more attention to Douglas, and no one should doubt that he could defend himself. Trudeau should never appear to be running scared, I insisted. He should stick to presenting his own positions, criticizing the opposition only when obvious weaknesses could be exploited, particularly on constitutional matters, where both Stanfield and Douglas repeatedly floundered. I doubted that the debate actually mattered all that much. Lalonde came round to this view and agreed that pressure should be put on Douglas to stay at home by sending Eric Kierans to campaign in the NDP leader's riding. That strategy was adopted. No doubt Tommy Douglas had won the great debate, but his electors rewarded him with defeat on election day.[15]

While I rarely participated in strategy discussions, I remember being consulted by Lalonde on one other matter that eventually proved very important and about which my advice was utterly unsound. One morning he told me that the organizers of the Montreal St-Jean-Baptiste Society parade on 24 June had invited the prime minister to sit in the reviewing stand. Everyone expected that his presence would cause an uproar. Still, Trudeau and his friends had come to Ottawa to raise the French Canadian profile. To refuse to show the federalist colours at a nationalist celebration would be tantamount to surrender. What did I think? Like most of Trudeau's advisers – though not Lalonde – I thought that a confrontation with the nationalists the day before the election would be a risky provocation. Find a "prior engagement," I urged. Obviously, I did not know Trudeau as well as I thought. He went, stood his ground when the missiles began flying, and certainly won votes for his stubborn courage. In his friend F.R. Scott's, words (in another context):

Pierre, suddenly challenged,
Stripped and walked into the rapids ...
A man testing his strength
Against the strength of his country.[16]

By St-Jean-Baptiste Day, my job had ended. The primitive campaign flow chart on Lalonde's office wall noted for 25 June, "Burn the papers and run." So I thought I should get out early, and in order to reach Morden, Manitoba, to celebrate my parents' fiftieth wedding anniversary, I left Ottawa on 21 June. I had written one final speech, a victory speech. (We were optimistic.) If Trudeau was defeated, I told Lalonde, he was on his own. Lalonde thanked me warmly for helping and wondered if I would like to come back permanently to the Prime Minister's Office if Trudeau won. I was committed to Harvard, I told him, but maybe I would be interested later. Before leaving, I played prime minister one last time: I wired anniversary congratulations to my parents, signed Pierre Elliott Trudeau.

It was from Morden, on election night, that I reached Lalonde by phone. We laughed and congratulated one another. He said that Trudeau sent his thanks and hoped we could celebrate together before too long. Now that the campaign was over, with the election resoundingly won, I realized that Trudeau had proved all the skeptics wrong. He was a champion campaigner. But what interested me most was the way he had slipped into this unfamiliar role so readily and without becoming someone else. Pierre Trudeau, Liberal politician and prime minister, was still Pierre Trudeau, intellectual and friend. Having won a majority for the Liberals, he could remain his own man. After the leadership victory, Blair Neatby, who knew about prime ministers, said that Trudeau would need his old friends once he discovered the isolation of power, especially as some of his new friends would leave him on discovering that he was not a miracle worker. Perhaps, I thought, and of course I hoped he would need his old friends. But I also knew, beyond doubt, that Trudeau's strength came from inside himself and not from public approval or even the flattery of his friends. Trudeaumania had not changed that.

THREE

A FRIEND IN POWER

By "patriotism" I mean devotion to a particular place and a particular way of life, which one believes to be the best in the world but has no wish to force upon other people. Patriotism is by nature defensive, both militarily and culturally. Nationalism, on the other hand, is inseparable from the desire for power. The abiding purpose of every nationalist is to secure more power and more prestige, *not* for himself but for the nation or other unit in which he has chosen to sink his own individuality.

GEORGE ORWELL, "Notes on Nationalism," 1953

THE HARVARD YEAR

After six exciting weeks in the corridors of power, I looked forward to returning to the quiet of academe now that my country was in such good hands. Work on my volume in the centennial series, the Laurier-Borden years, had been too long delayed, and I also had to prepare courses for the year I was to spend at Harvard. Having become a Liberal supporter, it seemed more appropriate than ever that I should become the second Canadian to occupy the Mackenzie King Chair of Canadian Studies, succeeding Claude Bissell. Trudeau, who had spent a year at Harvard as a graduate student, had asked me several times about what I was planning to do in my courses. I usually replied that when I stopped writing his speeches I could start figuring that out. As usual, he urged me to concentrate on my "important work." Ottawa was tempting, but I was glad of the Harvard excuse. I was worried about my unfinished book and was committed to my recent decision to move to York University to help start a new graduate program in history.

We spent part of July in the Neatbys' house in Ottawa while they were on vacation. I worked at the Public Archives and did not see any of my powerful friends, who also were on vacation while I was in the capital city. Although this was disappointing, it gave me an opportunity to think about the previous months and to begin reading the instant books that soon began to appear on the Trudeau phenomenon. Over the next year, I prepared a review of some of these books for the *Tamarack Review*. At Harvard I gathered some interesting new information about Trudeau's graduate student days there. (I was also asked to encourage the near alumnus who was now prime minister to accept a Harvard honorary degree. He declined; he would accept one from a small French-speaking college in the Maritimes instead. That filled the year's quota.)

Quincy House, under the mastership of Eleanor's former teacher Charles Dunn, became our Harvard home in late August. Harvard – in fact, Cambridge, as a whole – was a fairly riotous place and became more so as the year wore on. Stereos boomed out of the residence windows, frisbies flew across the quad, and hippies wandered the streets, long-haired and sandalled. The U.S. election was at full throttle: Richard Nixon vs Hubert Humphrey. Occasionally a car would pass bearing a bumper sticker reading, "Why not Trudeau here, too?" I certainly didn't lose touch with events at home. The *Globe and Mail* arrived several days late, but the *Montreal Star* could usually be found in Harvard Square on the day of publication. Reading my old friend George Ferguson's paper became a habit. *Le Devoir* I read in the comfort of the Widener Library.

During the term, a series of Canadian visitors came to the Kennedy Center, invited by Robert Bothwell, who had been my student in Toronto and was now my teaching assistant. (I'd never had one before, now I had three.) These visitors included

Carl Goldenberg, now a senator and Trudeau's adviser on the constitution, who spoke about the reform process; Gérard Pelletier, with Robert Rabinovitch and André Ouellette as executive assistants, who gave a fine survey of recent changes in Quebec; and David Depoe, perhaps Canada's leading hippie and at least for a time a Trudeau enthusiast, who offered ramblings on youth politics. Meanwhile, through my daughter Maggi's school, the Bilingual School in Belmont, I made contact with a wonderful French Canadian diplomat named Pierre Trottier, his wife Barbara, and their two sons. Trottier was an External Affairs officer whose most recent posting had been Paris, and he was now on study leave at the Center for International Relations at Harvard. He was a poet of established reputation, a fascinating storyteller, and something of a Gaullist. We struck up a close friendship, though he revealed a surprisingly negative attitude to federal French Canadians. These Canadian connections kept me up to date.

Although most of the Harvard faculty showed little interest in Canada (not so surprising, with an election and the Vietnam War in progress), there was one exception. The political scientist Louis Hartz had written about Canada in his *The Founding of New Nations* and, on my nomination, had spent a month as a centennial visitor at the University of Toronto in 1967. He took me under his wing, and I learned that he had shared a graduate seminar with Pierre Trudeau – "little Pierre," as little Louis called him. They had not been close friends, but he remembered Trudeau as quiet and unassuming. Not a potential prime minister, but certainly a potential scholar.

At the end of October I returned briefly to Canada, travelling first to Toronto to speak to a student group concerned about French-English relations, on to another talk at the University of Western Ontario, and then to Ottawa for my first conversation with Trudeau since the election in June. On the way I met Jim Davey on the plane. He told me that things were going well; also that he had visited Herman Kahn's Hudson Institute and been impressed with its forecasting about the future of technology. Davey was a born technocrat, too easily impressed by the idea that science could be applied to politics.

The next morning I dropped in on Marc Lalonde, who looked rested and relaxed; the tension of the spring had vanished. He told me that at Premier Daniel Johnson's funeral Trudeau had had a frank talk about Canada-France relations with the French foreign minister, Couve de Murville. The Frenchman had said he found Trudeau *trop logicien* in contrast to his own *réalisme*. Lalonde also said he was puzzled about the English Canadian agitation favouring the attempted secession of Biafra from Nigeria, a theme that Trudeau would take up at lunch. Then he showed me the operations room (Jim Davey's invention), which I described this way: "A fantastic room – locked with a combination – where Pierre's life and the government's legislation is programmed … it is an attempt to set down a programme for the next four years, down to the last speaking engagement. It has a kind of science fiction aspect – but worse it cuts Pierre up into little boxes. Poor man." I don't know what happened to this attempt to take chance and fun out of politics, but I do know that soon many things happened that no one had managed to squeeze into a box.

At 12:45 PM I went to the Prime Minister's Office, as I recorded in my notes on the visit:

Pierre came out of his office, dressed in a black corduroy suit, and soft black loafers. He looked harassed, but other-

wise fit and not too tired … We went down to the car. The
conversation began at once.
"Where shall we start?" he said. "Tell me about Harvard."
So I gave him [my] feelings about the signs of disintegration
and violence in the U.S. He was very interested. Arrived at
his house. I had Dubonnet, he had nothing until lunch when
he ordered a small amount of Dubonnet. (We ate spinach
pancakes, fruit and coffee, the latter on the back lawn).
He wanted to talk more about violence, which he said concerned him, more and more. Said he had remarked during
a cabinet discussion of NATO that the way things were going
in the Americas, it might appear ten years hence that governments should have been concentrating much more on domestic questions than on other things like NATO. His one worry
about getting out of NATO appeared to be that it might contribute to isolationism in the U.S. (Later he implied that he
would like to see all of our NATO contribution converted
to Biafran aid.)[1]

But Biafra puzzled him too. Why the outcry in English
Canada when his government was doing everything possible
in a complicated situation? I said, rather unthinkingly, that
it was his Boer War: "The English Canadian Protestant con-
science was at work shouldering the white man's burden again.
He took this up at once, and said he would use it. I said, for
god's sake no, it would just annoy people. But he likes to
annoy!!!!" He seemed to like my suggestion that he speak to
Cranford Pratt, but I don't think he ever followed up.
    Then we turned to the experience of governing, which he
seemed to be enjoying, though he fretted about the slow pace
of parliamentary debate. Reform of the rules was obviously on

his mind. Then he remarked that the one thing that really frustrated him was "that he was never ahead of the game, but always just keeping up. I said I was sure that no p.m. had ever been ahead of the game. He shot back typically, 'I would like to be the first.'"[2]

Afterwards we returned to his Centre Block office so that Michel Vennat could brief him for Question Period. We shook hands and, as always, he sent his best wishes to Eleanor. I made this assessment: "My overall impression was of a man very much in control, a man who has not even begun to call on his immense inner resources of energy. In the House in the afternoon he was the man in charge, fielding questions, knowing when to give a serious answer, when to avoid the barbs of another, when to put the questioner down (as he did with Dief, twice), and when to be witty. Though the government seems more "centrist" than I had anticipated, I think it will be a very good government. Moreover as Jim Davey said one year is not going to produce much that is new – but years 2, 3 and 4, should be very interesting."[3] Little did I know!

Back in Cambridge I couldn't quite escape from Canadian affairs. Bothwell's visitors continued to come, and Nixon's election seemed to stimulate my students' interest in Canada. On one occasion, a young man from New York City even asked about the chances of homesteading in the Peace River district. I had no need to ask why he was interested. Another student, Ken Glazier, a dual U.S.-Canadian citizen, would soon be required to choose one or the other. He asked for a reading course in Canadian affairs (and became our child sitter). He turned out to be what was called a "student leader" at Harvard – they seemed to be anointed rather than elected – and through him I had an inside view of the student turmoil when the strike was called in April. So the talk about Canada with students and younger historians was often more about the present and future than the past.

In February, just before a powerful winter storm closed the Cambridge-Boston area for a few days, I flew to Ottawa to do a running TV commentary on the federal-provincial conference on the constitution. This was the first of several in which I joined Charles Lynch, Norman DePoe, and Lloyd Robertson, filling in the blank airspaces while the provincial premiers consulted one another about the price of wheat, timber, cod, or provincial diplomatic representation abroad. The federal government, skilfully led by the new prime minister, pressed on according to the planned sequence: charter of rights first, division of powers later. The provinces made a variety of efforts to divert the discussion, especially when it focused on what they might be willing to do to implement minority language guarantees. Constitutional conferences on television, while necessary in the age of participatory democracy, were hardly the best stage for fruitful bargaining. One day, after waiting an unusually long time for the provincial leaders to return from lunch, I asked the prime minister over an open line – though it was not going out to air – whether they had been wining and dining. "Not much wining," he replied, "but a great deal of whining." I thought Charles Lynch would choke.

Before returning to Harvard after the February 1969 meetings, I had lunch at 24 Sussex Drive with Trudeau and Lalonde. An illustration of the wonderful relationship between the prime minister and his principal secretary came as we finished the first course. "Shall I keep my fork?" Lalonde asked. "You think this is some cheap French restaurant?" Trudeau replied. Marc laughed more heartily than any of us. The conversation was mainly about the recent conference and the hope that some progress had been made. Trudeau made it plain, once more, that his intention was to win adoption of the charter of rights that he had set out in his paper at Charlottetown.

"THE COPS ARE COMING!"

Returning to snow-clogged Harvard, I resumed academic work and watching Ken Dryden of Cornell shut out the Canadian-dominated Harvard hockey team. But it was hard to concentrate, mainly because the campus was caught up in the debate over Vietnam, the draft, and especially the presence of the ROTC (the student Reserve Officers Training Corps) recruiters on campus. The same debates, plus the issue of "African studies," had erupted at many U.S. universities. They were mild at gentlemanly Harvard where the Students for Democratic Action were present but weak. (I read every issue of their newspaper, *The Old Mole*, avidly. Henry Kissinger, then at Columbia, was "hungry," one published, purloined administrator's letter reported, twenty-five thousand would get him.)

Then, in an unusually intense fit of that exuberance that infects students in the spring, the main administration building was occupied to protest recruiting on campus. Very early one April morning, as students ran through the corridors of Quincy House, I thought I heard the cry of "The British are coming, the British are coming!" Once awake, I realized that these student Reveres were actually shouting, "The cops are coming!" Indeed they were. I went out to watch the arrival of the Massachusetts State Troopers, clad in powder blue, armed with riots sticks, revolvers, flak jackets, and Plexiglas visors. Very eerie. The occupation was quickly ended, but a lengthy student strike followed. All this was highly exciting and at times amusing for a visiting Canadian with nothing much at stake – though it was tense at times, even for us. At one point I told

Eleanor that I would send her and the children home if violence erupted in Roxbury, Boston's depressed black neigh-
bourhood. I attended the faculty meetings, and my student
Ken Glazier and a black student were actually allowed to
speak, hoping to explain the concerns of the strikers. Glazier
was a bit overawed by his surroundings, but the black student
spoke with the eloquence of Martin Luther King. However,
President Nathan Pusey abruptly cut him off when his brief al-
lotted time ran out, and he politely took his seat. The strike
soon collapsed as classes (which had never been cancelled)
filled up again.

My predecessor Claude Bissell had been deeply influenced
by the growing violence on U.S. campuses the previous year
and thought he saw it coming to Canada. I was less certain, as
I had told Trudeau at our recent lunch, for our students did
not face the draft or the racial tensions that were creating the
black power movement. As events turned out, both Bissell and
I were wrong. English-speaking campus violence didn't amount
to much, though there was a new radicalism at many universities, predictably taking on a nationalist guise. But in Quebec,
a noisy radicalism that mixed nationalism with a heady brew
of Marxism and Third World rhetoric – picturing francophones as *les nègres blancs d'Amérique* and federalists (*fédérastes*)
as *rois nègres* – won support from some students and a few
union leaders. Much of their abuse was directed at the unsym-
pathetic, indeed hostile, Pierre Trudeau.

NATIONALIST OR PATRIOT?

Leaving Nixon's troubled United States proved easy enough,
though the year at Harvard had certainly been a stimulating
one. In early 1970 I set out my rather gloomy thoughts in a

submission to the House of Commons Committee on External Affairs entitled "Look Homeward, Angel." The social and racial unrest in the United Stated convinced me that the Nixon administration would be preoccupied with domestic issues. My submission concluded, "Robert Frost was wrong: good fences do make good neighbours – especially now that our neighbour is likely to be spending more time in his own backyard." The polite questioning ended after an MP from Prince Edward Island asked if I agreed that island civilizations were superior to continental ones. Harvard had failed to supply the answer.

Coming home meant watching the Trudeau government at closer quarters and occasionally talking with my now eminent friend. We spent a few weeks in the Gatineau that summer, but Trudeau was out of town most of the time, and I had only one conversation with Marc Lalonde, who was his usual cheery self, now settled into his role as Trudeau's alter ego. Lalonde, whose importance in Trudeau's political life has never yet been accurately measured, took charge of tactics while Trudeau concentrated on strategy. The 1972 election, "the land is strong" election, would demonstrate that the "thinker" role alone for the prime minister did not work. Moreover, the Liberal organization outside Quebec remained something of a mystery to both the prime minister and his principal secretary. Lalonde's decision to run for Parliament in 1972 opened the prime minister's office to a new group of powerbrokers, led by Keith Davey and Jim Coutts, who were more at home with the party machinery in the rest of the country.

"The days of wine and roses," as Roméo LeBlanc dubbed the first Trudeau years, had only just begun in the summer of 1969. I had the feeling that after the completion of the reassessment of foreign and domestic policies which the new government had initiated, Trudeau's own approach to governance would emerge. In the meantime, I had a new teaching position at York University; my anthology of translated documents on French Canadian nationalism was about to appear; and I had a review of several instant books on contemporary Canadian politics to write for *Tamarack Review.*

My review in the end was harsh. None of the writers – Peter Newman, John Harbron, and Patrick Nicholson, among others – had done much homework. Don Peacock's *Journey to Power* got most of the story of Trudeau's rise right; I somehow missed Martin Sullivan's *Mandate '68*, the best of the bunch as I realized when he sent it to me later. Having recently participated in an election whose outcome many commentators had attributed to Trudeaumania, I used the opportunity to question the politics of personality that television in particular had nurtured. I objected to "the kind of journalism that views politics as nothing more than a clash of personalities, for it reduces public life to the level of the late night movie. The gladiators joust and the crowds, urged on by our syndicated columnists, cheer wildly. As the performers tire and occasionally stumble, the commentators snarl and the crowd grows dissatisfied. Soon the cry goes up for new players."[4] Trudeau himself had benefited from the voters' thirst for new faces.

Behind this comment was, of course, my realization that Pierre Trudeau could not possibly live up to the expectations that Trudeaumania had raised. Among his 1968 supporters, I had met young Quebec nationalists, far-left NDPers, and, most frequently, journalists and even Liberal politicians whose understanding of Trudeau's antinationalist federalist philosophy and commitment to bilingualism was founded on little more than a few hastily read newspaper articles. Only Edith Iglauer of the *New Yorker* seriously investigated Trudeau's pre-political life in an effort to understand what that magazine cleverly called "Prime Minister/Premier Ministre."[5] The departure first of Paul Hellyer and later James Richardson from the Trudeau cabinet were cases in point. Hellyer admitted that he had not read *Federalism and the French Canadians,* while Richardson apparently lacked any understanding of his party's stand on official languages. The fact that much of Trudeau's intellectual production was in French made it a foreign country to most English-language journalists, even those who bothered to read. It was only a matter of time before disillusion set in among those whose image of Trudeau was constructed from personal imagination or yearning.

EXPLAINING TRUDEAU

Over the next year or so, I wrote several essays and did one translation that made more of Trudeau's intellectual makeup available to those readers who turned the cornflakes box round when confronted with French. One of the first essays in my anthology *French Canadian Nationalism* was a long excerpt translated from Trudeau's introductory essay in *La grève de l'amiante.* This anthology had been in the works since well before Trudeau took power, but the translation now explained to a wider audience the reasoning behind the new prime minister's antinationalism, though many still thought or hoped that this attitude applied only to Quebec. Next came a request from the Prime Minister's Office for a translation of an essay that had appeared in 1944 in a publication unknown to me, *Jeunesse étudiante catholique.*

"L'ascétisme en canot" revealed in a unique fashion an aspect of Pierre Trudeau that had drawn me to him almost from our first meeting – his self-discipline. In this beautiful, deceptively simple essay, composed at twenty-five, he wrote: "To remove all the useless material baggage from a man's heritage is, at the same time, to free his mind from petty preoccupations, calculations and memories. On the other hand what fabulous and undeveloped mines are to be found in nature, friendship and oneself! The paddler has no choice but to draw everything from them. Later, forgetting that this habit was adopted under duress, he will be astonished to find so many resources within himself." Here was no mere canoeist in a fringed buckskin jacket – a later popular image – but a member of a canoeing expedition, one for whom thought and action were one. This short essay revealed much of the essential Pierre Trudeau.

Eleanor and I set about making the translation. It proved difficult. Although we had translated Trudeau before, the style and content of this piece were personal and compact, and being little more than recreational canoeists, we found the experience unfamiliar. (One word, *escousses,* utterly defeated us.) We did our best, but as I learned later, it was not quite good enough. Tim Porteous was given the task of making the rough places plain. The last paragraph especially fascinated me, for in the French version Trudeau had written that he knew "a man whom school could never teach him nationalism but had acquired that virtue when he felt again in his flesh the vastness of his country and when he experienced in his bones how great had been the creators of his homeland" (my translation). Nationalism a virtue? Had this youthful Pierre Trudeau been in hiding until now? (I knew, of course, that he had shared the nationalists' opposition to conscription during the war.) When I returned the finished translation, I asked Porteous for a favour: "Ask Pierre," I wrote, "if the man referred to in the last paragraph is the present Prime Minister!"[6]

Trudeau's answer eventually arrived. First, he thanked us: "For many years we have been proclaiming our belief in the theory of bilingualism. I appreciate your help, as always, in practicing it." Then came his response to my queries: "To answer two questions raised in your letter, the word "*escousses*" is an old French form of "*secousses*" [jerk forward] which has survived in French Canada, and I was describing myself in the final paragraph." In brackets he scribbled, "As if you had not guessed!"[7]

When the translated essay appeared in *Wilderness Canada*, a book dedicated to the journalist Blair Fraser who had drowned on a canoeing expedition, I discovered a second, momentarily disconcerting answer. Trudeau's "nationalism" had become "patriotism," and "*la patrie*" ("homeland"), a nationalist term, had disappeared completely.[8] Was a youthful dalliance with the sin of nationalism never to be admitted now that he had found the true antinationalist faith? I never asked because, after rereading the essay, I realized that he had not changed fundamentally, but his understanding of the essential nature of nationalism had deepened. (Trudeau's transformation, it is now evident from the research of Esther Delisle, Max and Monique Nemni, and John English, was more radical and astonishing than I had realized or easily accepted – from Catholic nationalist and separatist in the late 1930s and early 1940s to anticlerical, antinationalist federalist by the end of the 1940s.)[9] The more he observed and studied nationalism in French Canada and elsewhere, the more he understood that ethnic homogeneity is at the heart of nationalist ideology. His feeling for "the vastness of the land and the greatness of those who founded it" lacked the necessary ethnic reference required to qualify as a "nationalist." "Patriot" accurately described his sentiment.

In a remarkable essay on patriotism and nationalism, entitled *For Love of Country*, Maurizio Viroli drew exactly the distinction that Trudeau had made when he discreetly changed "nationalist" to "patriot" in 1969. "The language of patriotism," argued Viroli, "has been used over the centuries to strengthen or invoke love of the political institutions and the way of life that sustain the common liberty of the people, that is love of the republic; the language of nationalism was forged in late eighteenth-century Europe to defend or reinforce the cultural, linguistic, and ethnic oneness and homogeneity of a people."[10] These lines describe almost perfectly the difference between Trudeau's mature vision of Canada and that of nationalists inside and outside Quebec. Those who later claimed that Trudeau's insistence on a charter of rights and his rejection of every effort to identify the Province of Quebec with the francophone nation made him a Canadian nationalist, failed to understand this subtle but fundamental distinction.

Since Trudeau's political success had made *Federalism and the French Canadians* a runaway bestseller (whether or not every buyer found the erudite discussions of the virtues of federalism engrossing), the search was soon on for a successor volume. Jacques Hébert, Trudeau's longtime comrade-in-arms, gathered together a series of newspaper pieces that Trudeau had written for the reform journal *Le Vrai* in the late 1950s and published them as *Les cheminements de la politique*. In these popular articles Trudeau presented some lessons in liberal political philosophy, democracy, and popular sovereignty – part of his effort to overcome what he had already described as "obstacles to democracy in Quebec."

Ivon Owen of Oxford University Press, a neighbour of ours, decided to issue an English translation and invited me to write an introduction. This gave me a chance to do some research into a part of Trudeau's past about which I had only a slight understanding: the period when he and others worked unsuccessfully to create a non-party coalition of all the anti-Duplessis groups in Quebec. Somewhat to my surprise, I found that

Trudeau had been much more active politically than I had suspected. This man was hardly the ivory-towered intellectual that he had appeared when he decided to run for Parliament. Moreover, the failures of these early political activities provided an essential clue to Trudeau's decision to join an established party – and one he had often criticized severely – when he chose the Liberal Party in 1965. (When his government upheld an embargo on the sale of Canadian uranium to France and Stephen Roman of Denison Mines appealed to him to raise it, arguing that he had been a Liberal all his life, Trudeau replied coolly, "I haven't!") Writing this introduction, which Professor Trudeau graded "a brilliant piece" (but only after Professor Lalonde had corrected my deficient Latin),[11] convinced me that I should read all of Trudeau's early writings, or at least whatever I could find. There was obviously quite a lot that I had missed.

Naturally, *Cité libre* was the first place I looked. I had done an extensive random reading already, but now I turned the pages one by one, amazed at the variety of material published there: the first appearance of Anne Hébert's magnificent poem "Le tombeau des rois," for example, and Jeanne Lapointe's essay interpreting French Canadian literature. Then there was Jean Le Moyne, who in 1960 defined his position and that of many *Cité libristes* like this: "Mon héritage français, je veux le conserver, mais je veut tout autant garder mon bien anglais et aller au bout de mon invention américaine. Il me faut tout ça pour faire l'homme total" ("I want to keep my French heritage, but it is just as important for me to keep my English chattels, and to go to the limit of my American gift of invention. I need all that to make the total man.")[12]

Another position in *Cité libre*'s camp would lead down a different path. Pierre Vadeboncoeur, an essayist whose antinationalism matched or even exceeded his friend Trudeau's in the years before 1960, together with Fernand Dumont and Marcel

Rioux, all later became convinced separatists. Gérard Pelletier's contributions, numerous and subtle, introduced me to a journalist of clarity and balance, and later helped me understand why this self-effacing man was so essential a part of Trudeau's life. In 1985 my friend the historian René Durocher, a nationalist of the ambiguous sort, and I shared a car with Pelletier following a Canadian Studies conference in Germany. After Pelletier dropped us off, Durocher confessed that he had never realized what an obviously honest intellectual this federalist was. Pelletier found political life much less comfortable and satisfying than Trudeau, and gladly exchanged politics for a short but important diplomatic career before returning to his first love, writing.

I realized from this careful reading of *Cité libre* that the magazine had not, as was sometimes claimed, been simply a vehicle of Trudeau's personal views. Certainly he was at the centre of the intellectual action, but he was first among equals, not more. His contributions were often outstanding – rigorously thought out, tightly written, and passionate. I decided that a collection of these articles in translation would display the many-sidedness of his intellect, reveal why he was reluctant to engage in root-and-branch constitutional reform, and show what he thought about other important matters of public policy. For instance, some would be surprised to discover that as early as 1958 he had been concerned about U.S. domination of the Canadian economy. Such a collection of essays would also document his passion for democracy, his trust in the people, and his distrust of elites, especially clerical and nationalist elites, who claimed to speak for the people but rarely tested this claim in democratic waters.

After selecting a large group of these essays, I sent them off to Jim Bacque at Macmillan. He had edited my *Canada and the French Canadian Question* (which my Montreal publisher

Pierre Tisseyre, unannounced, had entitled *Le sphinx parle français*). Bacque had also edited my nationalism anthology and Trudeau's federalism book. But the new collection never appeared in print, despite my prodding. Perhaps the translation costs were prohibitive. Nevertheless, my work had been valuable to me, and I turned some of it into an essay on Trudeau. "Federalism, Nationalism, and the Nation-State" explained where Trudeau came from by setting out his main ideas. Many voters had been won by little more than charisma in 1968. I wanted to show that the new prime minister's real style was his intellect. Most reviewers of the book in which the essay appeared – *The Maple Leaf Forever*[13] – praised it generously, while my friend the historian W.L. Morton suggested that I was too much in awe of my subject and was more at home writing critically about my colleagues in the historical profession!

The book had what for me was a substantial sale in its first year. Although I would like to think the Trudeau essay was the attraction, a more likely explanation was probably the prominence given my book in an article by Sonia Sinclair in the Canadian edition of *Time*. Ms Sinclair, a Czech in origin, shared my reservations about nationalism generally, and the editors of *Time* may have welcomed my critical assessment of the Canadian brand. As I already knew, antinationalists, like nationalists, sometimes make strange bedfellows.

CIVIL LIBERTARIAN

Reading Trudeau's writings systematically convinced me that his decision to join the Liberal Party in 1965 had not been only an opportunistic strategy, though it had been the surest way to provide a federal counterweight to the nationalist thrust of

Quebec. But the decision was not entirely inconsistent with his past. Although he had always been a reformist and a supporter of trade unionists and other social activists, his philosophy was liberal, left liberal. He had often been associated with members of the NDP, such as F.R. Scott and Eugene Forsey, and had supported his friend Charles Taylor's NDP candidacy for Parliament, though he had never joined the party. And although his writings sometimes suggested that capitalism would evolve in a social democratic direction, he always emphasized that his goal was *la démocratie d'abord,* leaving social democracy for another time. That he was sometimes accused of being a communist or a communist sympathizer resulted mainly from his travels in the Soviet Union with identifiable leftists such as Madeleine Parent, or in Red China with that other innocent, Jacques Hébert. His failed attempt to row from Florida to Cuba in 1960 sprang from a physical rather than an ideological impulse.[14] During the 1968 election the rumour that Trudeau was a communist or at least a sympathizer circulated mainly in rural Quebec ridings where the Créditistes were strong, or in columns written by right-wing journalists, who in some cases were of Eastern European origin. Early in 1969, when David Slater, the president of York University, brought some faculty members and members of the Board of Governors together for dinner, I was seated beside Alf Powis, president of Noranda Mines – and our first and I think only exchange came when he turned and said, "I hear you know Trudeau. Is he really a communist?" My negative reply seemed to satisfy him.

Trudeau often seemed more leftist in foreign policy matters – notably his concern about the Third World and his opposition to nuclear arms – than in domestic affairs. Since his pre-1960 political focus had been on Quebec, it is hardly surprising that his preoccupation was to promote and defend democracy and civil liberties, essentially liberal causes. Taken together with his internationalism, this liberalism made him an antinationalist. It was on these issues that we shared so much common ground, though I was a card-carrying member of the NDP, indeed, a founding member. For me, social democracy and nationalism were opposites, and the CCF and its successor the NDP had always defended civil liberties.

My civil libertarian principles had been learned at United College in Winnipeg. There, in my final two years, I spent much of my spare time listening to, and usually agreeing with, Professor Harry Crowe. Almost daily we gathered at coffee time in Tony's, the college coffee shop. Harry, a semi-permanent cigarette drooping from his mouth (when lit, ashes dropped unnoticed onto his lapel and tie), would regularly bring his listeners up to date on the evils of Senator Joseph McCarthy. His colleague Ken McNaught was often present to add his acerbic analysis of the Great Republic. Not surprisingly, having drunk deeply at this fountain of radical liberalism, my first foray into letters-to-the-editor writing was a critical response to a law student's defence of McCarthyism in the *Manitoban*, the student weekly.

Those coffee-hour discussions led me to propose to Arthur Lower, in the fall of 1954, that I write my master's thesis on some aspect of the history of civil liberties in Canada. He suggested that I study the War Measures Act and civil liberties during the Second World War. Until then I hadn't realized that the subject existed, but over the next year the Defence of Canada Regulations, issued under the War Measures Act (1914), became my daily fare. In the course of my research, which included a study of the Winnipeg Civil Liberties Association that Lower had founded, I interviewed many of the critics of the regulations: M.J. Coldwell, F.R. Scott, Andrew Brewin, Glen

Howe the Jehovah Witnesses' lawyer, and, of course, Lower himself. My completed thesis, entitled "Canadian Freedom in Wartime, 1939–45," sharply criticized the Mackenzie King government's cavalier disregard for such traditional rights as freedom of speech, freedom from arbitrary detention, and assumption of innocence.

My conclusion recommended the replacement of the War Measures Act with a more limited piece of security legislation and the enactment of a constitutional bill of rights to prevent any repetition of such wartime injustices as the arbitrary removal and attempted deportation of Canadians of Japanese origin. Lower didn't mind that this study of the past offered practical proposals for the future. The thesis research served at least two purposes. It convinced me that I should continue my education as an historian by entering the PHD program at the University of Toronto, rather than joining the Department of External Affairs or entering law school. Second, it furthered my education as a civil libertarian with a special interest in the War Measures Act. It was in these same years that I discovered Pierre Trudeau's writings, though that irony only occurred to me in October 1970.

Harry Crowe's dismissal from United College by the Board of Regents for opinions expressed in a private (and filched) letter in 1958 once again stimulated my concern about individual freedom – in this case, academic freedom. I also carefully followed Glen Howe and F.R. Scott in their separate fights for religious freedom and against the Padlock Law and other legislation in Quebec. Their legal battles further strengthened my civil liberties principles and my conviction that the country needed a bill of rights. In 1960, on CBC radio and in the *Canadian Forum* I criticized Diefenbaker's Canadian Bill of Rights for its lack of teeth – it was a mere act of Parliament rather than a constitutional amendment. When the Conservative attorney general of Ontario, Sam Cass, proposed to give the Ontario Provincial Police arbitrary powers of search and arrest, I denounced him in a CBC commentary that ended with Thomas Jefferson's admonition that the tree of liberty required frequent watering with the blood of tyrants. (This prompted a neighbour in Morden to phone my father, asking, "Did I hear that your eldest son had been in Cyprus?" "Yes," my father replied, "with the UN peacekeepers." "I heard your younger son on the CBC this morning," the neighbour jokingly responded, "I expect he'll soon be in Siberia!") My efforts to be appointed to the board of the Toronto Civil Liberties Association were disappointingly unsuccessful. I could have been of some use at least as an historian; in October 1970 the executive director Alan Borovoy, speaking on CBC-TV, admitted that he had no idea that the War Measures Act was still on the statute books. Not surprisingly perhaps, I had never discussed civil liberties or the War Measures Act with Pierre Trudeau. I had simply assumed that we were in full agreement.

AN EXCELLENT ECONOMIST

In the early months of 1970 events seemed to be moving in a promising direction. In the Quebec provincial election in April, the Liberals, under their youthful new leader Robert Bourassa, were victorious. I was slightly acquainted with Bourassa. In the spring of 1969 Alfred Hero, the director of the Boston Council on World Affairs and the father of one of my daughter's schoolmates, had asked me for the name of a French Canadian provincial politician or journalist who might agree to speak to the council. He told me he could neither get a reply from René Lévesque nor a specific commitment from Claude Ryan. I suggested that he try Bourassa, who was the Liberal's rising star and likely to become the next leader.

As things turned out, Bourassa wasn't much of a star that day. After giving his carefully prepared written presentation, he had great difficulty responding to the rather uninformed, but hard-headed, Boston businessmen who had gathered to hear him. Pierre Trottier, Louis Duclos, Canada's deputy consul in Boston, and I occasionally jumped into the breach. The following day we lunched with Bourassa, and afterwards, as we strolled along the banks of the Charles River, he announced that he intended to run for his party's leadership. "Could I defeat René Lévesque?" he asked. Someone replied, "Lévesque is a wonderful speaker." Bourassa shot back, "I am an excellent economist. I can become a wonderful speaker, but Lévesque will never be an excellent economist." All of us laughed, including Bourassa, though I was skeptical.

His self-confidence stood the test. First he won the leadership, then he triumphed over the recently established Parti Québécois, talking mainly about economics – jobs. I wrote to congratulate him and received a friendly reply. Early in May 1970 I spoke to Marc Lalonde, who was in Toronto trying to sell Finance Minister Ben Benson's progressive tax reforms. (He wasn't having much luck, but the West was even tougher, he said.) He was pleased with Bourassa's victory, he told me, and even happier that Paul Gérin-Lajoie, an advocate of radical constitutional change, had asked too high a price for Bourassa to take him into his cabinet. (He wanted the deputy premiership and the Ministry of Intergovernmental Affairs.) Then Lalonde told me that the federal Liberals had made sure that Lévesque suffered personal defeat in Laurier, something that Bourassa had bridled at, thinking it better to have Lévesque in the legislature. The provincial Liberals, Lalonde suspected, wanted Lévesque personally elected as a threatening symbol that would strengthen their position in constitutional negotiations, but he himself thought that the only harmless separatist was a defeated separatist.[15]

Obviously the relationship between the two Quebec Liberal parties was far from what Trudeau and his friends had hoped back in 1965 when they planned their triple democratic coup: control of the federal Liberal Party (achieved by Trudeau's leadership victory), election of a Liberal majority government (achieved on 25 June 1968), and finally, control of the provincial Liberal Party. (That probably was to have been Marchand's role and reward.) But the last step proved impossible. Bourassa, who had once collaborated with Lévesque in drafting his *Option Québec*, was far from accepting Trudeau's version of federalism.[16] Events, however, soon forced them together, but only temporarily.

FOUR

LIBERTY INFRINGED

L'autoritarisme est la tentation du pouvoir; l'alarmisme, celle
de l'opposition.

GÉRARD PELLETIER, *La crise d'octobre*, 1971

ENTER THE FLQ

Throughout the 1960s Quebec had echoed with furious debate
while the rest of Canada, at least occasionally, attempted to understand if this signified anything. Forty years later it is hard
to recreate the atmosphere, which was alternately confusing,
exciting, frustrating, and boring. Of course, unrest in Quebec
was far from unique. Most of the industrial world had experienced various degrees of tumult; the events that shook Paris
and Prague in 1968 were spectacular examples. Cities burned
in the United States, and university campuses erupted with
demonstrations and "non-negotiable" demands. In the remains
of the colonial world, from North Africa to South America,
verbal and physical violence, terror, and repression became com-
monplace. Gillo Pontecorvo's film *Battle of Algiers*, which I saw
for the first time with my friend Carl Berger sometime in late
October 1970, caught the temper of the times brilliantly.

Some of the most powerful and revolutionary anticolonial
writing appeared in French, works such as Franz Fanon's *Les*

damnés de la terre (prefaced by Jean-Paul Sartre) and Albert Memmi's *Le portrait du colonisé*. They circulated in radical nationalist circles in Quebec. Pierre Vallières, who with Charles Gagnon briefly succeeded Trudeau and Pelletier at *Cité libre*, applied these ideas to French Canadians in his *Nègres blancs d'Amérique*. Another though somewhat paler imitation of these francophone North African anticolonial theorists arrived in my mailbox in mid-October 1970. Autographed "avec mes hommages," Léandre Bergerons's *Petit manuel d'histoire du Québec* came in a tricolor dust-jacket of green, white, and red, the flag of the Patriots of 1837, with a yellow star in the upper left-hand corner, symbol of the Front de libération du Quebec. His accompanying letter told me that additional copies could be obtained from the Canadian Liberation Movement in Toronto.[1] Bergeron (like me a displaced Manitoban) had previously denounced me in a book review in the leftist *Canadian Dimension*, so I was a little surprised by the almost friendly tone of his letter. For a brief moment I wondered what the RCMP might think of this evidence of my association with a terrorist movement.

Violence and the rhetoric of revolution, part of university campuses everywhere, had grown increasingly shrill on the fringes of the Quebec independence movement by the mid-1960s. The FLQ, in imitation of national liberation movements abroad, set off large and small explosions in post-office boxes and on federal property, causing substantial damage and killing at least three innocent French Canadians. Trudeau's election did nothing to appease these radical nationalists, and perhaps it even infuriated some of them. Bourassa's 1970 triumph over the Parti Québécois, and the charges that questionable means (the "Brinks affair") had been employed in the Liberal sweep, doubtless intensified the anger of those who had already decided that "bourgeois democracy" would never bring justice to "the white niggers of America."

That anger and ideology led to the kidnapping of James Cross, the British trade commissioner in Montreal, on the morning of Monday, 5 October 1970, marking the beginning of what will doubtless always be known as the October Crisis. A "manifesto" stating a series of FLQ demands, including the release of what they called "political prisoners" (members of the FLQ who had been convicted of armed robbery, bombing, and other crimes), gained wide publicity and even some support. Most of their demands were rejected, the Trudeau government adopting what I believed was the correct, firm line (though the manifesto was broadcast, as demanded, and negotiations were tentatively suggested).

Then a second kidnapping, this time of the Quebec minister of labour, Pierre Laporte, was successfully carried out on the afternoon of Saturday, 10 October. Every day the press reported demonstrations and speeches supporting negotiations with the kidnappers. Suggestions that the Bourassa government should recruit reinforcements from other parties or independent public figures circulated in Montreal and Ottawa. Mayor Jean Drapeau and his deputy, Lucien Saulnier, to say nothing of the Créditiste leader Réal Caouette, issued dire warnings, while the Bourassa government issued sometimes contradictory statements from its "bunker." On 15 October, as turbulence and fear grew and the police searches produced no results, the Quebec government requested military support. The federal government dispatched the army. Troops in the street in Ottawa, Montreal, and Quebec increased the atmosphere of crisis. During this period I attended a conference at

McGill on the theme, appropriately enough, of war and society. The sight of armed soldiers on the streets of downtown Montreal – not a great many, but some – left me depressed.

But the worst was yet to come. In response to increasing pressure from Bourassa and Drapeau to provide further assistance in the unsuccessful and exhausting police search, the Trudeau government proclaimed the War Measures Act at 4 AM on 16 October. Pierre Trudeau, my civil libertarian friend, had resorted to the use of a piece of legislation that I believed should long since have been erased from the Statutes of Canada. The following afternoon, the FLQ cell holding Pierre Laporte reacted by murdering him. I was *bouleversé* – bowled over.

> The blood-dimmed tide is loosed, and everywhere
> The ceremony of innocence is drowned. (W.B. Yeats)[2]

BEWILDERMENT

What did Laporte's murder mean? The most obvious possibility was that the crisis was more threatening than even a close Quebec watcher in Toronto could perceive. Why, I wondered, had the police been so inefficient? Was the Bourassa government collapsing? Had the War Measures Act killed Pierre Laporte? Would James Cross be next? One question that never entered my mind, then or later, was: Had Pierre Trudeau been corrupted by power? Trudeau's political enemies, some Quebec nationalists, the Parti Québécois, and especially those farther to the left began to develop various conspiracy theories. These usually centred on the claim that the real motive behind the proclamation of the War Measures Act had been a desire to discredit the PQ. One conspiracy theory that I heard attributed to an academic sociologist at Laval even held that Ottawa had acted on orders from the CIA. I remained persuaded that Trudeau's public statements, while doubtless incomplete, represented a transparent explanation for this drastic action. None of the books hastily pulled together by anglophone journalists and intellectuals – Aubrey Golden, Ron Haggart, Denis Smith, and others – changed my mind. Only Louis Fournier's *F.L.Q.: The Anatomy of an Underground Movement*, published fourteen years later, came close to an accurate description of the context of the events of that doleful October, and even it is based on limited documentation.

While I trusted Trudeau and accepted that the federal government had responded to requests from the premier of Quebec and the mayor of Montreal, based on the belief that an "apprehended insurrection" existed, I remained doubtful about the necessity for this action. Even though he had to answer directly to Parliament the day the War Measures Act came into effect (something Mackenzie King had avoided for nearly a year in 1939–40), the extent of the suspension of civil liberties – searches without warrants and preventative detention, arrests without bail and without laying charges – made me very uneasy. Perhaps the existence of a widespread revolutionary network would soon be revealed, or at least the kidnappers and murderers would be captured. Maybe that would convince me.

My emotional turmoil and intellectual confusion during the first few days of living under an act that I had so carefully studied and condemned was intense, the more so because I feared that my friendship with Pierre Trudeau hung in the balance. I had no personal fears, but I was momentarily upset when my close friend Viv Nelles asked if being such an identifiable Trudeau supporter did not cause me some concern about my safety. Utterly surprised, I replied in the negative. Later I phoned Eleanor to suggest that we might pay more than our usual attention to the comings and goings of Maggi and Mark, both of whom travelled some distance to and from the Toronto French School.

When I returned to the university following the weekend of Laporte's murder, I faced the challenge of making up my mind and stating my position in public at a time when I found most of my colleagues in a state of confusion equal to my own. A request from a group of highly agitated students that I speak at a War Measures Act rally forced me out of my uncomfortably ambiguous cover. The attitude of the students greatly surprised me. They wanted to rally support for the Trudeau government's action, obviously believing that Laporte's death demonstrated the strength and seriousness of the revolutionary forces in Quebec, a power that could destroy Canada. I had expected them to represent York's small student radical movement, which was spouting the usual quasi-Marxist clichés in *Excalibur*, the student newspaper. (I had forgotten that students largely ignore student newspapers.) I reluctantly agreed to speak, unsure of what I would say, though realizing that my invitation came from students who expected me to support their views.

On the day of the rally, several thousand students congregated around the ugly ramp leading up the front of the ugly Ross Building. (At lunch we sometimes speculated that the Ross Building had been constructed for an adaptation of the Battle of Algiers, the York Liberation Movement students rushing up the ramp only to be repulsed by buckets of boiling oil poured down from the Administration's offices on the ninth floor.) I can't recall who spoke first, probably Dean Jack Saywell who, with his usual good sense, expressed general support for the Trudeau government's actions but urged a calm, wait-and-see attitude. I was next, if memory serves. I, too, urged calm but indicated that I was unconvinced by the evidence so far presented by the government for such drastic action as the implementation of a piece of legislation that had long offended me. What, I asked, could justify the arrest of the popular Quebec singer Pauline Julien? (In 1968, when the singer had appeared uninvited at the conference of francophone nations in Niamey shouting "Vive le Québec libre!" I had been rather less sympathetic to her.)

The crowd, expecting more rousing leadership from their professors, began to grow restless. Jack Granatstein, then in his radical phase, roundly and forthrightly denounced the federal government for its authoritarian action, thereby giving the students something to shout about. He was loudly and lengthily booed. That made me, born a minoritarian, deeply uncomfortable. Thirty years later Granatstein recanted, while my doubts have continued. Not long afterwards I attached my name to a statement calling for public hearings on the government's conduct and a repeal of the War Measures Act. Although I had left the NDP, I admired its consistency in its defence of civil liberties, even though I knew that two significant figures in the party, F.R. Scott and Ken McNaught, publicly supported Trudeau.

As it became increasingly evident that the proclamation of the War Measures Act had become a major item in the Quebec nationalists' and separatists' campaign to discredit Trudeau and federalism, I lapsed into silence. Jacques-Yvan Morin, Michel Chartrand, and others toured various parts of Canada spreading the anti-Trudeau message, while René Lévesque and even Claude Ryan took every opportunity to argue that Trudeau had hijacked Quebec and taken Robert Bourassa prisoner.

Gradually I came to believe that the government's best defence was the argument that the War Measures Act was the only emergency legislation available, and that it had to be used. Even then, one could ask, as I did: Why not special legislation freely debated in Parliament before implementation? I later learned that some members of Trudeau's cabinet, including the prime minister, initially favoured this position but feared that the parliamentary debate would drag on unendingly. Bourassa and Drapeau wanted immediate action.

From the first October days, there had probably been more criticism of the federal government's management of the crisis by English Canadians than by francophones. The invocation of the War Measures Act intensified that criticism especially from intellectuals and some journalists. The *Canadian Forum*, where my translations of Trudeau's essays had first appeared, stood firmly by its half-century-old tradition as a defender of civil liberties. James Eayrs and Ron Haggart in the *Toronto Star* and George Bain in the *Globe and Mail* continually expressed doubts about the weapons chosen to fight Quebec terrorism. On the left (NDP) and the new left (the Waffle and various Marxist variants), where the appeal of Canadian nationalism had increased during the Vietnam War, sympathy for Quebec nationalism led to distrust of Trudeau and all his works.

ON GREY CUP WEEKEND

Doubtless recognizing the need to explain himself to his intellectual peers, and hoping perhaps to convince at least some of them that his actions in the continuing kidnapping crisis were justified, Trudeau had Tim Porteous call and ask me to arrange a meeting between the prime minister and his Toronto intellectual friends and critics. The choice of guests was left entirely to me. The gathering was to take place at my house following the Grey Cup game on 27 November. Eleanor and I agreed without hesitation, indeed with enthusiasm.

A good seminar should never be larger than a dozen or so participants. I invited an even dozen, not counting Eleanor and myself. Six I thought supported Trudeau's position with various degrees of certainty, and six were critics. Only Trudeau's harshest critic, Abe Rotstein, declined to join the party. The meeting, I had explained, would be private and the names of the participants would remain confidential. Jim Eayrs, not long after the evening's discussion, mentioned it in his *Star* column, while others have since spoken about it privately. My dear friend Eli Mandel, who had a long, intense exchange with Trudeau that evening over the relationship of violence to civilization, later recalled it in a poem entitled "Political Speech (for PET)":

> if the revolution was about to occur
> would the people of Quebec rise up
> the people of Quebec would rise up
> therefore the revolution was about to occur
> wrong again[3]

On the morning of the meeting, Porteous called to say that the prime minister wanted us to know that security would have to be laid on. If that made us uncomfortable, the gathering could be moved to Trudeau's hotel. I asked Eleanor, and she saw no need to move unless the meeting place became public. At 8 PM two plain-clothes RCMP officers, one French, one English, arrived at the front door. Neither was the officer who had been attached to Trudeau in 1968 and had run my security check. One politely asked if the back door was locked and requested that they be informed if any "strangers" arrived at the front door. They then retired to the second floor, refused radio and TV, and spent the evening, unknown to our guests, reading the newspapers. About 10:30 that evening, in the middle of the proceedings, Eleanor blew a fuse by plugging in the coffee urn, but the upstairs lights were unaffected and the Mounties stayed put. Downstairs, Trudeau continued to speak while we searched for the fuse box in the pitch-dark basement. The others fell abruptly silent until the lights were restored. We later learned that there were additional policemen stationed nearby, including at least one in the back garden. The neighbours were quite impressed. When Ken McNaught arrived bearing a box of rattling dinky toys for Mark, a policeman showed a modest interest, but no search or arrest was carried out. McNaught dined out on this story for years.

Trudeau had arrived about 8:45 PM, still dressed in the attention–catching cloak and slouch hat donned for his unimpressive official Grey Cup kickoff. I welcomed "the masked bandit." The kids waited on the stairs with Mara Teitelbaum. Pierre spoke to them in French asking how they were." Maggi, by now fully bilingual, giggled; Mark replied "bien." Then into the bear pit. But that is a misnomer. The evening's discussion was polite and even stiff at the beginning. Strong differences emerged several times, but there was never any acrimony. One clear memory is that the prime minister's strongest critics, both before the meeting and after, said very little. Nor did the group spend the whole evening on the War Measures Act. Discussion touched on Africa (French involvement in Biafra and trade with South Africa), economic policy (Trudeau was delighted to hear that President Nyerere of Tanzania had once asked for a one-handed economist so that he could get unambiguous advice on economic matters), national unity (Trudeau said his willingness to be flexible stopped at "special status" for Quebec), western alienation, and much else.

Naturally, Trudeau's response to the FLQ provoked most comment. That was why we had gathered. Trudeau defended his action, while admitting that, with hindsight, some things might have been done differently. He argued that he had acted on the advice of the Quebec government and not, as was being claimed in Quebec, vice versa. He had wanted a committee to oversee police activity, but Bourassa had refused. Trudeau went on to admit that the Public Order legislation allowed for "fishing expeditions." Both government and police, he said, were inadequately informed about the extent of terrorist organization in Quebec, and consequently the police sweep had been wide and unsystematic. In response to suggestions that reform of the RCMP was needed, he replied that a new commissioner from the outside had already been appointed, over much opposition. He insisted that the RCMP retained his full confidence and remarked that its impenetrability to infiltrators resulted from its stringent recruitment and training demands, especially horsemanship!

The exchanges were forceful and clear. The prime minister demonstrated his capacity to get to the heart of occasionally windy questions and comments, to answer questions in order, and to remember much later in the evening who had first raised what issue. Only once did he reply in a somewhat sharp way. A newspaper columnist complained that the emergency measures had led to editorial censorship of his writing. Trudeau replied that an honourable person would have resigned in protest. Those who came opposed to the proclamation of the War Measures Act left with their opposition challenged but unchanged; the supporters doubtless felt reassured; and the ambiguous – me – remained ambiguous.

There was also a good discussion of Quebec. Trudeau explained his commitment to keeping the country together in a fashion that surprised some of the group, though certainly not me. He remarked that national unity was not divinely ordained and that the country might break up someday. But the federation was far better for French Canadians than separation would be. He said that in the past he had sometimes played an intellectual game in which Quebec separated, so that people would see how much better off they had been in Confederation; but now that he was a politician with responsibilities for the people, he no longer played this game. In this discussion I observed, as I had during the election campaign and later did in the constitutional debates, that Trudeau revealed a powerful identification with "the people." He had a sense that on matters such as separation and even the War Measures Act, the people's judgment could be trusted. That, of course, was the essential message of *Approaches to Politics*, and also what motivated his attempts to speak over the heads of journalists and other elites when he wanted to explain his actions. Although the press often cast him as an intellectual elitist (whatever that may mean), his whole career, from the fight with Duplessis to his attempt to provide for an appeal to the people as part of the constitutional amendment process demonstrated a powerful populist impulse. Conservatives, such as Professor W.L. Morton, recognized that Trudeau's political philosophy did not conform to the British tradition of parliamentary sovereignty. But in Trudeau's view, popular sovereignty, like parliamentary sovereignty, had to be restrained by constitutionally entrenched civil liberties.

Throughout the evening Trudeau sat upright in a straight-backed chair, intellectually alert and physically fit. He drank ginger ale, and towards the end of the evening he ate sparingly. His focus was always on the discussion, which he treated as an exchange among equals. He obviously enjoyed the give-and-take. (Porteous told Eleanor that the previous evening Trudeau had met with a group of businessmen to discuss taxes and had obviously been bored.) Although he was expected that night at a Liberal gathering at the home of his cabinet colleague Barney Danson, he stayed with the discussion until after midnight, despite several calls from his disappointed expectant host.

As the meeting was breaking up and goodbyes being said at about 1 AM, Trudeau remarked that Eleanor had been expecting a child on one of his earlier visits with me in Toronto, another example of his memory and his thoughtfulness. As the big black car (parked outside all evening) rolled up, he thanked us for "a glimpse" of the children. Then I realized that there were three cars, two for the police, one for the prime minister. Security had obviously been heavy. One of our guests returned to say his Rover wouldn't start. Eli and I gave him a push. Too bad Trudeau had departed; he could have witnessed the way the other half lived.[4]

Albert Breton, who was at our house for the November discussion, told me many years later that Trudeau had concluded after our meeting that the Toronto intellectuals were as impervious to his reasoning as their Montreal counterparts. Further meetings would be futile. He never told me that. "I was glad to be with some old friends whom I see only rarely these days, and that certainly includes the Cooks." He ended his letter of thanks, "I hope there will be other opportunities to get together before too long."[5] We certainly continued our discussions.

WAS THE REVOLUTION ABOUT TO OCCUR?

I never discussed our Grey Cup party with Trudeau or, for that matter, with the other people who participated, except in passing. The prime minister thanked us for "assembling and provisioning that scholarly company." He added, "I found the evening very lively and enjoyable, although I doubt that many convictions were shaken or opinions reversed." He observed that it was remarkable "how different the same country can look when viewed from Montreal, Ottawa, or Toronto."[6] Neither then nor later did I know quite what to make of this remark for it implied, somewhat uncharacteristically, that opinions and convictions could be explained by geography. It suggested that his critics would have concluded otherwise if they had lived through the crisis in Montreal. Perhaps. F.R. Scott had supported the government's action. But there were also many critics of that action in Montreal, just as there were supporters in Toronto and elsewhere. The comment likely revealed how deeply the October Crisis affected Trudeau, even though he would never admit any second thoughts about his decisions.

In response to a reported "apprehended insurrection," he had done what he had believed necessary: proclaimed the War Measures Act. Consequently, the "apprehended" never become "real." Could it have? How can anyone know if the "perceived" insurrection had been squelched? That, in my mind, had always been the essential defect of the War Measures Act; it left "apprehended" undefined. What a government "apprehends" as insurrection may look less threatening to others. The controversy over the October Crisis will never end, since there will always be different assessments of the relationship between "apprehended" and "real" insurrection. On that point, though no one articulated it, there was no agreement when the prime minister and my other friends met and debated on the night before my thirty-ninth birthday.

In January 1971 I received a long letter from Jim Davey who, though I was unaware of it at the time, directed the Strategic Operations Centre that devised and implemented the federal government's response to the crisis. Davey said he had seen my name on a pamphlet criticizing the use of the War Measures Act and wondered if that represented my views. The pamphlet, entitled *Strong and Free: A Response to the War Measures Act,* contained eleven brief articles that questioned, in fairly measured terms, the Trudeau government's action. Over sixty highly respectable citizens, including Claude Bissell, Lloyd Axworthy, Dalton Camp, Pauline Jewett, and Gordon Fairweather, signed it. Not surprisingly, those who suggested that the government had some ulterior motive in invoking the War Measures Act – an idea Davey pronounced "preposterous" – especially irritated him. He insisted that the depth of the crisis in Quebec, a crisis that was not simply the FLQ actions but was a profound crisis of authority, had to be understood very broadly. Only a powerful defence of the rule of law, of legitimate authority, could shore up a deteriorating situation and prevent the rot from spreading. He offered a revealing parallel:

But what is the balance sheet of the Quebec crisis? Over 400 people were arrested and put in prison for various periods of time, which is clearly something that no one is very happy about. But there were no people killed in the street, and there are no martyrs to the Quebec cause, where there might well have been. You, as a historian, know very well what would be the symbolic importance of the four or five CEGEPs kids [community college students] "killed in the cause of Quebec." Remember what happened after four such kids were killed at Kent State. Over 400 people were arrested and several have complained of various kinds of abuse. That kind of treatment is not condoned, but what is remarkable is that during this very tense situation the control of the authorities and the police was such that there was not considerably more.[7]

I knew that Trudeau had been concerned with the possibility that social unrest might lead to the same kind of violent situation that other countries were experiencing. He had questioned me about unrest in the United States. He had read a piece I wrote in *Le Devoir* commenting on Hannah Arendt's *On Violence*. Quebec in the 1960s and 1970s was in a state of convulsion whose outcome was unpredictable. The FLQ crisis demonstrated that. But was the War Measures Act the best, the only possible emergency response? I replied to Davey saying that I understood that my information about the crisis in Quebec might be deficient and that the seriousness of the situation required a firm response. But the powers provided by the War Measures Act were almost inevitable invitations to abuse. Did the magnitude of the threat equal the magnitude of the response? I needed more evidence. Not a harsh word was exchanged, nor did I feel any pain in my arm. If Davey discussed this exchange with Trudeau, either before it took place or subsequently, I was not informed of it.

During the next few weeks, and since, I have thought a great deal about the determined defence that Trudeau and Davey offered for the federal government's response to the FLQ terror.

Repeatedly I have re-examined the main arguments. I accepted their assessment of the seriousness of the challenge which the three levels of government had faced, and I thought that, for an outsider, I knew Quebec very well. But had the War Measures Act been the only recourse? Had special legislation with more limited provisions for search and arrest been given thorough consideration? Marc Lalonde, in the final issue if *Cité libre* (Fall 2000), said that cabinet documents revealed that Trudeau, when first faced with the proposal that the War Measures Act be proclaimed, maintained that existing laws were sufficient. Special legislation also was considered but was rejected because its rapid passage was too uncertain. In the end, the cabinet decided to resort to the War Measures Act and Trudeau agreed, but he "certainly wasn't the one who pushed for it."[8]

The arbitrary powers provided by the War Measures Act unfortunately did not lead to a quick resolution of the kidnappings: Laporte was murdered, and Cross remained in captivity until 3 December. Doubtless, the threat of this arbitrary power made it plain to those playing with revolution that the consequences could be serious, and this helped to restore a sense of security to the streets of Montreal. There was no Kent State. Moreover, Trudeau had faced his critics, both in the House of Commons and in parts of the press, in a way that sharply contrasted with the King government's persistent avoidance of parliamentary scrutiny during the Second World War. Always willing to give Trudeau the benefit of the doubt, I nevertheless remained and remain a skeptic: measures not men, my master's thesis research had taught me.

Gérard Pelletier, a man utterly without an authoritarian bone in his body, went as far as I could go, sometimes. He called the policy he supported *la solution la moins mauvaise*.[9] That, for me, summed up the October Crisis. But the politics of *la moins mauvaise* had not been what my long friendship with Trudeau had led me to expect.

The occasion for our next meeting, following another surprise decision on Trudeau's part, was a very happy one.

LIFE AFTER THE OCTOBER CRISIS

When on 5 March 1971 the newspaper headlines announced the unexpected marriage of Pierre Trudeau and Margaret Sinclair, like most people I was taken completely by surprise. Pierre's private life had never held more than a passing interest for me, though it had been difficult, in the period leading up to his election victory in 1968, to avoid all of the newspaper gossip. Although he often inquired about the well-being of my family and always sent greetings to Eleanor, I never interpreted these courtesies as invitations to inquire into his personal affairs. He obviously enjoyed the company of interesting, glamorous women, though his right-wing opponents had spread vicious rumours about the man who had legalized homosexuality. He certainly conversed with Eleanor and other women as his intellectual equals. (The night of our Grey Cup seminar, he and Eleanor had exchanged views on some obscure aspect of the life of St Thomas Aquinas.) Having once argued half seriously that Ward's Law ensured Trudeau's political success, I wondered in passing how marriage would affect his political career. Who could have guessed?

To celebrate the marriage of the prime minister, the governor general and Mrs Michener held a splendid party at Rideau Hall. It was very obviously a party for Pierre's friends, as Margaret would later note, understandably a little resentful. Friends apparently meant people he had known for at least a decade, so we barely made the cut. That qualification probably explained Mrs Michener's slightly weary question as Eleanor and I passed through the reception line: "And you're from Montreal too, I suppose?" She seemed relieved to learn that the prime minister had at least a few friends from the true centre of the Canadian universe. The ten-year cut-off, of course, meant that politicians were rare: Jean Marchand (who proved to be the star of the dance floor, Eleanor being greatly impressed), Gérard Pelletier, and a few others. Our table included Vianney Décarie, a professor of medieval philosophy, and his wife Thérèse, a brilliant psychologist. The friendly conversation, much of it naturally about Pierre and his new wife, revealed the loyalty of his friends towards him and nothing about their thoughts on this latest "sign of contradiction," the phrase Vianney had once applied to his wife's one-time suitor. Pierre circulated among his friends, obviously a happy man, happy with his bride, and happy to be with people who had remained his friends, even though he had now radically changed his life a second time.

That evening I formed no particular opinion about Margaret. When we danced, perhaps forewarned about my ballroom reputation, she asked me to dance slowly. We talked a little stiffly about common acquaintances at Simon Fraser, her alma mater. Martin Robin, a left-wing sociologist, had especially impressed her. She seemed what she was – young, beautiful, and understandably a bit bewildered by the company she had unexpectedly joined. On later occasions, when Pierre and Margaret came to dinner in 1974 during our year in Ottawa or at Harrington Lake in the summers, her self-confidence had obviously grown. She certainly did not stand in awe of her important husband. But our meetings were rare, and I never really came to know her.

To expand the newlywed prime minister's knowledge of the Prairie West – and birds – we presented Pierre and Margaret with William Kurelek's painting, *Alouette in Manitoba*.

FIVE

RIGHTS AND FREEDOMS ENTRENCHED

The bravest are surely those who have the clearest vision of what is before them, glory and danger alike, and yet notwithstanding go out to meet it.

THUCYDIDES, *The History of the Peloponnesian War*

PREPARING FOR THE FINAL ACT

During the 1970s my contacts with Trudeau were irregular, but always stimulating and often highly entertaining. There was certainly an abundance of both wit and intelligence at a dinner Carl and Shirley Goldenberg gave for John Kenneth Galbraith and his wife in June 1972. (Galbraith and Goldenberg had been acquainted since the Second World War, when they had helped administer their respective governments' attempts to regulate inflationary wartime economies.) Eleanor and I travelled to Montreal by train, anticipating a wonderful evening with Pierre and Margaret, Frank and Marian Scott, Jean Beetz, and the two young Goldenbergs, Eddie and Ann. We were not disappointed. Scott, himself well over six feet, set the early tone when he looked up to the towering Harvard political economist and, with mock amazement, remarked, "My God, you *are* tall!" The spirited, wide-ranging dinner conversation certainly included inflation fighting. Wage and price controls would soon embroil Trudeau in controversy. After ridiculing Robert Stanfield's call for a "price freeze" during the

1974 election, he would adopt a similar policy in 1975, perhaps under Galbraith's influence.[1]

Sometimes our meetings were family affairs where there was always a central place for the children. During my sabbatical leave in Ottawa during 1974–75, Pierre and Margaret came to dinner one evening. Pierre came in his buckskin jacket. When he learned that Mark was taking judo lessons, a challenge match was arranged – yellow belt versus black belt – on the carpet of John and Marion Porter's living room. It ended with black belt defeated. It was not always that way. Once at Harrington Lake, Pierre challenged us all to an unfamiliar skill-testing game. A thick Styrofoam water ski or surf board with two-foot-shaped cavities floated beside the dock. Competitors were required to jump from the dock into the foot cavities and remain upright as long as possible. Only the boys, including the old boys, played. I was no match for Pierre, who started the competition, but Mark proved more than a match. Pierre challenged the judges, claiming he had won. Eleanor insisted that her son had triumphed, but Pierre was adamant. (Mark later revealed that he could have remained upright much longer but decided to fall when someone called him a show off.)[2]

That evening Pierre barbecued a roast, experimenting, he said, with a new piece of equipment which the National Capital Commission had insisted on installing. After dinner, on Margaret's suggestion, we tested a new motorboat, also provided by the NCC. Pierre drove, Margaret urged him to open the throttle, and the rest of us – or at least I – looked forward to our return to the dock. As we left about 9 PM, the Trudeau youngsters already in bed, Maggi shyly asked first Pierre and then Margaret for an autograph. They happily inscribed their names and good wishes on a sheet of 24 Sussex Drive notepaper, divided in two, one for each of their admiring fans.

Pierre Trudeau competes for the aquatic stand-up floating
championship, Harrington Lake, summer 1983

No visit to Harrington Lake, or Lac Mousseau as Trudeau always called it, was complete without some discussion of the state of the nation. In July 1976, remembered in the Gatineau as the drenched summer when the Hydro-Québec workers struck and the power failed every weekend, Trudeau was preoccupied with a more threatening strike, that of the air traffic controllers. When that crisis ended with a victory for the English-language pilots, Jean Marchand resigned in protest, and *les gens de l'air* went on the warpath. In the middle of dinner, Trudeau was summoned to the telephone. He returned in a state close to anger: Marchand had phoned to urge him to appoint Serge Joyal to the cabinet. The young backbencher was threatening to take up the cause of the French-speaking pilots in caucus. Unhappy as he was about the terms of a strike settlement that contradicted his bilingual principles, Trudeau was not, he said, "prepared to be blackmailed by any ambitious little nationalist." He had told Marchand to deliver that message. Neither the pleasures of domestic life nor the new barbecue had undermined his determination to run his show his way.

BOURASSA DECLARES HIS INDEPENDENCE

After the October Crisis, most of our conversations were about the constitution and on strategies for responding to French Canadian alienation from the federal government. Trudeau's consistent plan, one that I supported, was to press forward with bilingualism, implement a constitutionally entrenched bill of rights, reform such federal institutions as the Supreme Court and the Senate, and then deal with the division of powers on a case-by-case basis. In 1971, at Victoria, he nearly achieved exactly that. The Victoria Charter proposed a short list of rights, including language rights, limitations on the federal spending power, increased provincial power over social policy, the end of the federal power of disallowance, and a guarantee of three Quebec judges on the Supreme Court, appointed only after consultation. A flexible amending formula would have given a permanent veto to any province with 25 percent of the population (Quebec and Ontario) and regional combinations of other provinces. Attractive as these pre-conference proposals were, Bourassa, shortly before the conference, asked for more power in the area of social policy, and that led to lengthy, often closed-door discussions.

During the conference, I again participated in the live TV coverage that had now become a standard part of constitutional discussions. Being in Victoria that June as spring turned into summer was certainly not a hardship. Working with Lloyd Robertson was always a pleasure. He knew his subject, knew how to ask questions, and encouraged people to relax. Between sessions, we sat around with the tigers in the Bengal Room at the Empress Hotel, gossiping with journalists and public servants. André Ouellette interested me most. In 1969 this redheaded Quebecer had been Gérard Pelletier's executive assistant and briefly had responsibility for establishing bilingual districts and organizing the committee to supervise them. He had appointed me to the committee without asking, but I declined. (I didn't want any appointment, though I once floated the rumour that I was going to the Salt Fish Board – which sparked Doug Fisher to report that I was finally getting my reward as Trudeau's amanuensis.) By 1971 Ouellette had been appointed a deputy minister in Ed Schreyer's NDP government in Manitoba. He became a westerner overnight, now arguing vociferously that wheat prices, not language policy, should be the focus of federal government attention. His premier had already made this point at considerable length during the conference, as he probably felt compelled to do since all the opening speeches were televised. It took me a while to realize that while I was trying to extract secrets from government officials, they in turn were spinning me.

Since the main event, the negotiations over Quebec's demands for more power in the area of social policy, took place out of reach of the cameras, we often sat about for long hours waiting for something to happen. No wonder journalists gather in bars! In the end, Bourassa retired to his Quebec City tent to brood. A week later, he rejected the Victoria agreement, having collapsed under pressure from the nationalists in his cabinet, led by Claude Castonguay, the minister of social affairs. Castonguay, though never a separatist, made several major contributions to the continuing constitutional crisis over the next two decades. Claude Ryan of *Le Devoir* (for whom any Trudeau project was suspect), together with the PQ, backed the charge that Victoria simply did not give Quebec enough. As events turned out over the next twenty years of constitutional negotiations, the Victoria Charter was arguably the best set of changes that Quebec could have obtained, especially the amending formula, which rejected the idea that would later become so popular and paralyzing – equality of all the provinces.

Obviously, the partnership between Bourassa and Trudeau during October 1970 had been a fragile one. Trudeau, having followed Bourassa's advice in responding to that crisis, probably expected Bourassa to stay on side during the Victoria discussions. After all, the proposals were designed for Quebec, and much hard work had been done to get agreement from provinces, especially western provinces, who saw little in it for their constituents. But Bourassa had his own, always ambiguous agenda.

Although I did not speak with Trudeau in Victoria, several of his officials told me of his frustration with the Quebec delegation and his irritation at the dogged, morose Castonguay. When Bourassa turned his thumbs down, Trudeau was furious, publicly furious. Like many Canadians, he concluded that enough was enough for constitutional discussions. I agreed, arguing in a piece for *Saturday Night* that until Quebec came forward with a set of very specific and realistic proposals for constitutional changes, the federal government and the other provinces should tread water. And so they did for the most part – until they discovered that René Lévesque, a free style swimmer in contrast to the dog-paddler Bourassa, had cannonballed into the constitutional lake.

The failure of the Victoria Charter in 1971, following as it did the FLQ crisis, demonstrated that winning the Liberal leadership and then the election in 1968 was simple compared to governing. The electorate delivered the next blow. In the fall of 1972 the voters reduced the Liberals to a minority in Parliament, one that would be dependent on David Lewis and the NDP. "Our kind of Canada," Trudeau wrote to me, "is going to take some hard work to build."[3] Marc Lalonde was more despairing, at least at first, telling me that he could not understand why so many English Canadian voters had deserted Trudeau. I replied that many unhappy voters would return if the minority situation was handled skilfully. With the constitutional debate on the back burner during the next two years, the Liberal government was able to focus on questions of more immediate interest to the electorate outside Quebec, especially on such economic concerns as Canadian control of petroleum resources, an issue pressed by the NDP. The Liberal-NDP alliance gave birth to Petro-Canada. By 1974 many disenchanted voters proved willing to give Trudeau another chance, but

the new majority government had not long been in office before the constitutional question returned to the front burner.

THE RENÉ AND PIERRE SHOW: ACT ONE

On 15 November 1976 I went to Montreal to comment on the
Quebec provincial election returns for the CBC. The unthink-
able happened – a PQ majority. Like most observers, I was
caught off guard. During my summer in Quebec I had seen
much evidence of dissatisfaction with the Bourassa government because of its failure to settle such major industrial disputes as the Hydro strike, to deal effectively and fairly with
language policy, and to respond convincingly to repeated charges
of patronage and corruption. Still, a separatist victory remained
highly unlikely. My radio comments were, for me, unusually
tentative, especially when the anchor repeatedly asked me for
"English Canada's reaction." Once the results were final, I
headed back to my hotel in a taxi, riding through streets filled
with cheering Quebecers waving the blue-and-white *fleur-de-
lis*. "What do you think about your new government?" I asked
the francophone taxi driver. "I'll wait to see," he replied, "If
we don't like it we'll kick it out the next time." That quick answer delighted me, but not as much as what he added. "You
guys from Ontario don't need to worry," he said, "We're not
going to build a wall around the province. After all, we may
want to get out!" His no-nonsense attitude made it easier for
me later as I watched the joyful, unthreatening crowds singing
and dancing the night away.

A more sombre mood prevailed at the airport the following
morning. "Last night was a very bad night, Professor Cook,"
a striking-looking woman remarked unexpectedly. It was Jeanne

Sauvé, whom I knew only slightly, returning to Montreal from Ottawa. I agreed and asked if she had spoken to the prime minister. She and other ministers had spent the previous evening awaiting the election's outcome with him. "He is very disappointed," she said. The word "disappointed," rather than "depressed," struck me at the time; it sounded like Trudeau. I wondered if even his disappointment might have been tempered with a little satisfaction at Bourassa's fate. I didn't ask Mme Sauvé; we shook hands and went our different ways. Nor did I ever ask Trudeau, though I knew he took a low view of the man he disdainfully called "a hot dog eater." He also believed that if Bourassa had signed the Victoria Charter, the PQ would have remained in opposition for *la longue durée*.

The Trudeau government's response to the PQ victory was a standard one: appoint a task force. (These were once called royal commissions, but there had been so many that a new name was invented to disguise an old delaying tactic.) Neither of the retired politicians appointed to chair the inquiry, John Robarts and Jean-Luc Pepin, had a razor-sharp mind, but both exuded charm and goodwill. To meet the apprehended crisis, the conference circuit started up again. Ian Macdonald, president of York, decided that a national meeting at his university was in order, and he asked me to give the keynote address. Participants came from across the country, many of them, like me, veterans of the 1960s talk fests – for example, Claude Ryan and Solange Chaput-Rolland from Quebec. My speech outlined the background to the PQ victory and stressed the need to avoid rhetoric in favour of very specific proposals for responding to Quebecers' discontent. (At one of the discussion groups Daniel Latouche, a self-important separatist political scientist at McGill, described my remarks as nice fairy tales.)

John Robarts spoke in disorganized generalities about the goals of his task force. Solange Chaput-Rolland responded in frustration. She wrote to me a few days later, saying that after Robarts's windy speech she had no confidence in the commission.[4] By the time I received her letter, she had accepted an invitation to become a member.

Not to be outdone, John Evans, president of the University of Toronto, held his own conference. York's was in the spring of 1977; Toronto's was that autumn. Asked to sit on the planning committee and to make a presentation, I wondered if the University of Toronto had no Quebec experts of its own. Harry Eastman, George Ignatieff, and President Evans apparently thought not. After the PQ election, many Canadian social scientists and law professors realized the benefits of acquiring, or at least claiming to have acquired, knowledge of Quebec and of the Canadian constitution. These scholars, often innocent of the history of Canada or of Quebec or nationalism, devised fanciful schemes for constitutional change that bore little relation to Canadian historical or contemporary reality. Thomas Courchene's *Rearrangements* (1992), for example, approximated social science fiction. And then came the philosophers ...

The University of Toronto's conference had a more academic tone than York's, which had attempted to reach a broad public audience. My paper, titled "Nationalist Ideologies in Canada," argued that "ethnic" nationalism, whether French or English Canadian, had always led to conflict. I cited Quebec's Commission des droits de la personne, which had recently criticized Bill 1, the Lévesque government's first attempt to make Quebec officially unilingual: "We believe that the confusion between belonging to a cultural group and to a civil society is indefensible and, even more, eminently dangerous." Although I had underlined exactly this confusion in my references to the history of unlingual English-language legislation in western Canada, Edward Watkins, a former Conservative leader in Alberta, complained that, as usual, my paper ignored the West. Only Northrop Frye seemed to appreciate my reason for beginning my paper with a few lines from W.B. Yeats's "Meditations in Time of Civil War":

> We had fed the heart on fantasies
> The heart's grown brutal on the fare;
> More substance in our enmities
> Than in our love.[5]

Between conferences I made a small contribution to a philosophical response by the federal government to the new Quebec regime. In the late spring I had a call from Pierre Juneau, who was then working in the Privy Council Office, his attempt to join the Trudeau cabinet and active politics having been blocked by the voters in Quebec. He told me that he was writing a response to Quebec's Charter of the French Language, the long document that explained the PQ government's unilingual language policy. Juneau said that his document, an exposition of official bilingualism, had been placed before the cabinet, and Trudeau had raised questions about the historical sections and told Juneau to ask me to check them. So I did and helped shore up a somewhat shaky draft.

A National Understanding/Un choix national has never had much attention paid to it, which is too bad, because it is a document that sets out very clearly the concepts of language, culture, and nation that underpinned all of the Trudeau government's constitutional thinking. Lévesque and the PQ nationalists, in their

Charter of the French Language, insisted that language and culture were inseparably united, forming the essence of the Quebec nation. (This had been brutally clear in Bill 1, Camille Laurin's first attempt at language legislation, but it remained in diluted form in Bill 101.) Trudeau and the federal government adopted the view that language was a tool of communication that was separable from culture in a nation state that nurtured diversity rather than homogeneity. "We must separate once and for all the concepts of state and of nation," Trudeau had written in 1962, "and make Canada a truly pluralistic and polyethnic society." In 1967, in some "centennial cerebrations," I had described Canada as a country of many "limited identities" rather than a single "national identity." One sentence in Juneau's document reflected both of these propositions: "It is precisely the rejection of uniformity, the refusal to accept a homogenous view of themselves that constitutes the most authentic and widely shared experience of Canadians. The affirmation and preservation of differences, personal, social, local, regional, cultural, linguistic has consumed the minds and hearts of Canadians all through their history."[6]

This "civic" view of Canada was not the one that inspired the Pepin-Robarts Report when it appeared in 1979. Instead, it returned to the old and in my view outdated dualistic conception of Canada as a country of two founding peoples. This confusion was confounded by at least a partial acceptance of the Quebec nationalist claim that Quebec, not French Canada, was one of the two partners. It recommended that dualism be recognized in a number of fashions and that several decentralizing constitutional amendments be entertained. The recipe was hardly one that appealed to the Trudeau government. By the time the report appeared, I was a visiting professor at Yale

University. But as usual I kept a close watch on developments at home, and having quickly read the task force's recommendations, I wrote a highly critical letter to the editor of the *Globe and Mail.* It was published as an op-ed piece, drawing a certain amount of fire from various dualists. The political economist and nationalist Mel Watkins argued, with his accustomed logic, that if I was against the report it must contain much that was good!

TRUDEAU AS PHOENIX

My year at Yale, a place I enjoyed much more than Harvard (Yale, not New Haven) was crammed with academic and intellectual work. The atmosphere was stimulating, since many students (some of them Canadian hockey players, whom I often cheered on at Saarinen's wonderful "Yale Whale") and some faculty found the study of Canada valuable. Robin Winks, among many other things an expert on the history of the Blacks in Canada, had taught Canadian history to Yalees for years. Howard Lamar, a professor of western American history with Canadian connections, encouraged me to read widely in the history of the Native Peoples of North America and invited me to participate in an international conference on comparative frontiers at Seven Springs, a luxurious Yale retreat in Westchester County, New York. After I had contested a paper by Francis Jennings, a dogmatic U.S. historian, Lamar told me I would have to write a replacement paper for the forthcoming volume. This work kept me busy throughout the spring, just when the Canadian voters were rejecting Pierre Trudeau and giving the Progressive Conservatives enough seats to form a minority government. Joe Clark, the new prime minister, opposed

Trudeau's "rigid" federalism with the idea of "a community of communities," a phrase he almost certainly took from Vincent Tovell, who had used it to describe western Canada in a television series called *Images of Canada* on which I had worked. Patenting or abandoning "limited identities" began to seem a good idea.

By the time of our return home to Canada and our move to the cottage for the summer, Trudeau was off on a northern canoe journey, growing a rather anemic beard. He looked to me like a man preparing to leave public life, though he had written to me, in what sounded like a form letter, saying "I'll certainly do my best to be a good leader of the Opposition – for all Canadians." If it had not been for the obvious elation of Lévesque and the PQ now that their principal foe was disarmed, I would not have been unhappy. After nearly fifteen years in federal politics, almost ten as prime minister, Trudeau had earned a rest. Politics had never consumed him. He had earlier, with the other *colombes,* contemplated a few years in opposition to renew the Liberal Party. His years in power had surely erased this ambition. As for me, my Yale year had introduced me to something new and very exciting: aboriginal and environmental history. Getting on with this was what I wanted most, and my attention would be undivided if Trudeau retired to a monastery. But still there was that unfinished business of defeating Lévesque.

In August 1979 Lalonde called to say hello, and since he was in Ottawa I suggested that he come out to Tenpenny Lake to cool off. He looked very fit and happy for a man who had just lost an election. He relished the idea of doing battle with the new Clark government. His shadow cabinet portfolio as energy policy critic especially pleased him. The oil crisis was far from over, and he knew the energy issue would put Clark's people to a rigorous test, one that he was already preparing. I asked about Trudeau, and he said that he expected to see him back at work full-time after a few months of his old life and some self-examination. But wasn't the Trudeau government's defeat a windfall for the PQ, especially with the promised referendum fast approaching? It wasn't that obvious, Lalonde replied. Trudeau would soon begin his own campaign against the PQ's project. There were already plans being laid for an early provincewide tour, with Trudeau visiting schools, colleges, and universities – the usual hotbeds of separatism – to debate his nationalist opponents. Given his demonstrated effectiveness in these situations, this concentrated campaign would probably have more impact than the few brief forays his prime ministerial responsibilities would have allowed. Lalonde was always planning. Once again, I was impressed by the tough intelligence of this remarkable and good-humoured son of rural Quebec. But I was not totally persuaded.

Events, of course, did not unfold as Lalonde predicted on that warm August afternoon by the lake. In November, Trudeau announced his decision to resign from the party leadership, an announcement that really unsettled me. Don Macdonald would make a fine Liberal leader and prime minister after someone else had taken care of Lévesque. But what would happen to Trudeau's planned tour of the province, dissecting the PQ project? Maybe he would be even more effective, once more the freelance intellectual. Or maybe the nationalists would ridicule him, either as another *vendu* or, as Michel Brunet had once said to me of Louis St Laurent, just another French Canadian abandoned by the anglos once he had served their purpose. In any case, these worries were short-lived.

THE MEANING OF 14 MAY 1980

Trudeau's return to the leadership after he had resigned it, and his return to power after he had lost it, came in rapid succession in the spring of 1980. Thanks to Joe Clark's ineptitude – first as the prime minister who couldn't count and then as the party leader who couldn't campaign – Trudeau was back in office in time for the May referendum in Quebec. I was relieved. With the politically unskilled Claude Ryan in charge of the No forces, there could be no doubt that help would be needed. That help could now come from the Prime Minister's Office and from a prime minister whose whole adult life had been a preparation for this campaign.

Like most Canadians outside Quebec, I watched the referendum campaign as a bystander. I probably watched more of it than others who were not directly involved, following it through Quebec newspapers, radio, and TV, and constant conversations with friends. I heard many stories of Ryan's shambling campaign, where endless speeches were delivered in freezing hockey arenas, with the leader left to speak after the TV news crews had left to meet their deadlines. From the beginning, the Yes forces seemed to have the energy, the initiative, and even the edge in a close campaign. A *Oui* victory seemed even more possible after Lévesque began watering down his platform with qualifications and promises of additional popular consultations. Rumours that Jean Chrétien and Marc Lalonde were taking control of the federalist troops and that Trudeau was gearing up for a few star turns soon became welcome possibilities. Trudeau's intervention had become imperative.

In an early speech, Trudeau heatedly chastised Lévesque for suggesting that his Elliott name raised doubts about the authenticity of his commitment to Quebec. He had refuted this racist slur often enough. Then, on 14 May, a week before the vote, he delivered his most powerful, important, and influential speech, at the Paul Sauvé Arena. Taking a leaf from the book of Ernest Lapointe during the 1940 provincial election that brought down the Duplessis government, Trudeau stated, "I know because I spoke to the [Liberal] MPs this morning, I know that I can make the most solemn commitment that following a No, we will start immediately the mechanism of renewing the Constitution, and we will not stop until it is done. We are staking our heads, we Quebec MPs, because we are telling Quebecers to vote No, and we are saying to you in other provinces that we will not accept having a No interpreted as an indication that everything is fine, and everything can stay as it was before. We want change, we are staking our seats to have change."[7] The speech was cheered thunderously. Undoubtedly it made an essential contribution to the outcome of the referendum: nearly 60 percent refused Lévesque's request for a mandate to begin negotiations leading to sovereignty-association.

Anyone who knew Pierre Trudeau, anyone who made an effort to understand his fundamental ideas and had attentively watched his efforts to reform the constitution since 1965, would have understood the principles that would inform the fulfilment of that 14 May promise. He had repeated his goals ad nauseum for all to hear. Fundamental to his thought and action was his unshakeable belief that the federal government represented all Canadians, irrespective of cultural or ethnic origin. Any recognition of Quebec as the "national state" of francophones contradicted the essential principle on which Canada had been founded and would lead, willy-nilly, to demands for full Quebec sovereignty. If on 14 May 1980 there were people who heard Pierre Trudeau promising something that contradicted these repeatedly enunciated principles and policies, heard him promising to fulfill their fantasies about "special status," "distinct society" or "Quebec's traditional demands," the problem was with their ears and imaginations, not with what Trudeau said and unambiguously stood for.

Professor Guy Laforest made the best of an unconvincing case when he argued that the "context" of Trudeau's speech made his words mean something much more than his previous thoughts and actions had indicated – that he intentionally used the context to convince his audience that he meant something more than his known bag of constitutional tricks. Similarly, although Gordon Robertson, in his *Memoirs of a Very Civil Servant*, first claimed somewhat cautiously that Trudeau's speech "left the question later whether the voters had been misled about the nature of his commitment," he then, in his selective account of the 1987 Meech Lake Accord struggle, unambiguously and without the slightest supporting evidence described Trudeau as a man "who would so obviously mislead the voters of Quebec in his address at the Paul Sauvé arena in May 1980 during the referendum campaign and then charge them with misunderstanding what he had said." The claim is unconscionable. No one had more opportunity to understand Trudeau's principles than Gordon Robertson, who worked for ten years as his constitutional adviser and supported his decision to break unilaterally the constitutional deadlock in 1981. After all, Robertson played a major role in formulating the policies that followed from Trudeau's principles. He, more than most, surely knew that Trudeau was a man of firm constitutional principles. Later, after Trudeau declined to beg Robertson to reverse a retirement that he had pronounced "was not reversible," Robertson could only whine like a jilted suitor. Mackenzie King "did not himself understand Quebec," the omniscient Robertson wrote from his ouija board, but King "would have had no trouble with the concept that Quebec is a 'distinct society'"[8] This perfect self-description reveals nothing about Pierre Trudeau. He did understand Quebec, and he repeatedly risked his political career on that understanding.

Victorious in the referendum, Trudeau set out immediately to fulfill his promise. He knew that once Lévesque and his ministers regained their equilibrium they would be equally determined to prevent him from doing so. In his book *Désobéir*, Claude Charron, the youngest Lévesque minister, revealingly described the depression and utter confusion in the PQ cabinet after the disappointing referendum defeat. (The dominance of that mood may explain some of the Lévesque government's strategic failures in the 1981 constitutional discussions.)[9] Delighted at the outcome of the referendum, I looked forward to complimenting Trudeau personally on his up-to-standard performance even without my speech-writing assistance.

Before going to Tenpenny Lake for the summer, I wrote congratulating him on his referendum victory. The reply, addressed to "Mr. Cook," made me wonder why I had fallen from favour! Still, this form letter, as I supposed it to be, contained at least one revealing paragraph. After emphasizing his conviction that, in rejecting independence, Quebecers had also expressed a strong desire for constitutional change, he went on: "Their desire for change appears to be echoed in the rest of the country and I am confident that we will be able to take advantage of the historic opportunity that this has given us to provide Canada with a new constitution more in keeping with the needs and aspirations of all Canadians."[10] He obviously intended to fulfill his May 14 commitment quickly. In fact, he had already set the wheels in motion.

In August, on what turned out to be not an exactly typical day at Harrington Lake, I discovered his determination to succeed. Here are my notes (typos and spelling corrected):

Monday, August 11
Yesterday Pierre Trudeau phoned suggesting that we get together Monday or Tuesday. Said his kids were having friends out to Harrington for a swim and maybe if the day was nice we would like to join the fun. Otherwise maybe Tuesday. Left me to consider, saying we could decide Monday if day nice. He called again Monday morning and since the day promised to be hot, with Tuesday less promising, we decided to go. He added that a new element had entered the picture: Margaret, just back from London, would be there. He referred to her as "my wife," and said that if that did not complicate matters for us, it did not for him. I said it was no problem for us and that we would come. We were asked to be at the gate at Harrington at 1 p.m. since that was when the hordes would be there.

We obliged. When we arrived Pierre was on the lawn trying, not very successfully, to fly a kite-like object which Margaret had brought for Justin from London. He looked very well rested, tanned, a little stouter than when we last saw him in summer gear. He welcomed us enthusiastically. Margaret appeared – very friendly, I kissed her. She looked like herself – bluish pink shirt and slacks, purple shoes, something written on her T-shirt. They seemed relaxed. Soon a horde of very nice kids arrived. Pierre said time to swim and ushered us into the house to change – also gave us some wonderful Iraqi candy.

As usual he was splendid with all the kids – swam with them, horsed around, and challenged them to dive higher and swim faster. He and Mark had their usual wrestling match – on the suggestion of arm wrestling he characteristically replied he would like that – he had once been champion. Always a competitor.

At various points we talked. He was animated. Obviously entirely pleased to be back in office. Said he was very worried about the West. It was worse than Quebec had been since there were always defenders of federalism in Quebec but the West seemed to have only provincialists. Said that changes needed to be made to prevent the parties from being so regionalized. Tories deserved seats in Quebec, he deserved seats in the West. Otherwise he had no *political* mandate from West and found it hard to pretend to be a spokesman for all Canada. Said either PR [proportional representation] or US system would be better. I demurred loudly on latter. He said he wanted, and offered, a coalition with NDP – one with cabinet posts for them and an agreed program. It needn't last forever but would have given government some moral authority in West. Said Broadbent had appeared to agree but after talking it over with someone had come back and said he could not convince his party. Pierre thought Ontario NDP and CLC was the problem. Anyway, he said, they just had "no balls." He said it would have caused him just as many problems in his party as Broadbent would have had in his, but he was willing to give it a try.

Then, or at some later point after swimming, he turned to the constitution. Especially mad at Blakeney and Romanow. Said Blakeney played public role of "great Canadian," but in closed sessions he was narrow or worse than other western premiers. Said Romanow very narrow and unwilling to give in on language rights. I asked if he got on with Lougheed. Well, said Pierre, he is hard to hate, he is so earnest, so lacking in humour, so concerned about appearances. Duplessis at least had a sense of humour and didn't take himself so seriously. He could be hated – but not Lougheed who just wanted to do right by Alberta. Sterling Lyon, he said, was nothing but Lougheed's Charlie McCarthy.

Then he said he wanted to know what I thought about unilateral repatriation. Hasn't this country got at least that much will? he asked. If they wanted to be a loose community of communities, he said, that was not the Canada he believed in. His question caught me off guard. At first I waffled, but then I said why not go for unilateral repatriation. If this is really your last stand, why worry, you have nothing to lose. And surely there can't be too long a howl afterwards. He agreed – but referred to the flag debate. There would be a parliamentary debate that would drag on endlessly, preventing action on inflation, etc. But then he said but should we just repatriate or should we get some changes into the repatriated constitution? How about a Bill of Rights and language rights? This really threw me. [Mark told me later that he hadn't understood the question but he knew from the astonished look on my face that it was important.] I said that if infringement on provincial powers were included then the fight might be serious. He agreed without saying whether he wanted to fight or not. But he had clearly thought all of this over very carefully. (The leaked Pitfield [in fact Kirby] memo of a couple of weeks later substantiated all this.)

He was really in good form – full of interest in everything I said, Eleanor said. And wanted to know what the kids were up to and so on. He was so good with all the little kids – playful, warm and genuinely interested. As we left he put his hand on Maggi's red hair – after a discussion in French about her education – and spoke some admiring words. He had also won Mark's heart by agreeing to come to the Tenpenny Lake games if other demands did not interfere. He said his kids would like to see another lake. As things turned out, he was unable to come, and phoned his apologies."[11]

This conversation soon joined in my memory with the one we had engaged in at the Royal York Hotel in February 1968. I now knew that the plans were ready for the final push to achieve the goal that Trudeau had set for himself on entering politics in 1965, and to fulfill the forthright promise he had made at Paul Sauvé Arena on 14 May.

THE RENÉ AND PIERRE SHOW: THE FINAL ACT

Early in September the so-called Kirby Memorandum detailing the federal constitutional strategy became public. It confirmed what I had learned at Harrington Lake. A few weeks later the federal-provincial conference collapsed in the face of the conflicting goals of the various participants. Deadlock, which had been central to the PQ government's pre-conference strategy, was achieved. Trudeau's next step followed: the tabling in Parliament of a unilateral patriation resolution. Then came the expected long debate, one in which Joe Clark valiantly defended the provinces, allowing time for court challenges, followed by an appeal to the Supreme Court. That court's judgment, which I had gone to Ottawa to comment on with Dean William Lederman of Queen's University, was oracular: what was legal was not constitutional, the majority concluded. We commentators were left literally speechless, the Supreme Court's new TV sound system having failed.

Finally, there was the November conference, which again almost failed, even with Trudeau's continuing threat of unilateral action. Deadlock, and victory for Lévesque, loomed once more. Trudeau was ready: he challenged Lévesque to a referendum on the federal proposals (arm wrestling again). By accepting the challenge, momentarily, the Quebec premier broke the common front he had so carefully helped to construct. The fox, Claude Morin, could no longer control the chickens frightened off by Lévesque's misjudged bravado. Don Stevenson, a leading Ontario public servant, told me later that the Quebec delegation, so sure it could stop Trudeau with its "Gang of Eight" strategy, had come to Ottawa with no alternative, no fallback position. Trudeau had gambled and had won nearly all of the chips.

Agreement, without Lévesque, could now be reached on a patriation package containing a charter of rights that entrenched language rights – but at the price of a "notwithstanding clause" that allowed provinces to override unacceptable laws and court judgments, and an amending formula recognizing the equality of the provinces. Trudeau had gained the essentials he had outlined at Charlottetown in 1965, but it was not entirely his ideal constitution. The Victoria amending formula remained his first choice or, as a way of breaking future deadlocks, a referendum provision. He got neither. "As you know," he told me at the end of the long siege, "it is not quite the constitutional package I would have liked, but I respect the spirit of compromise that allowed us to find common ground."[12] And he had been wrong about Roy Romanow, who, with Roy McMurtry of Ontario and Jean Chrétien, had been a leading player in the final deadlock-breaking drama.

The November success and the eventual proclamation of the Canadian Constitution in April 1982 left me nervous about

Quebec, but happy that the long struggle had reached such a satisfactory outcome. With patience and luck, Quebec would gradually return to its usual cool realism. The PQ and Lévesque would now have to rethink their strategy, even their mission. In the process, the party would probably splinter into a modernized Union Nationale and a hard-line separatist faction. If constitutional debates were quietly adjourned for a decade or so, federal provincial conferences could return to normal, once again looking carefully at concrete reform proposals.

Trudeau had done his job brilliantly, doggedly sticking to the course he had set for himself when in 1965 he had decided to exchange his life as an independent intellectual for the constraints – and power – of party politics. At long last I could take my friend's persistent advice to concentrate on what is really important: studying and writing history. I confidently – too confidently – believed that an important chapter had closed. Perhaps now Pierre would return to his old life and we could resume our long-distance conversations.

SIX

FRIENDS

I have sometimes obeyed the powerful dictates of my heart, and given voice to my feelings; for as I do not pretend to be free from the weaknesses common to my fellow-creatures, it was necessary for every reader to know the colour of the glass through which I looked.

GEORG FORSTER, *A Voyage Round the World*, 1777

ALMOST THE LAST HURRAH

In April 1983 Marie Choquette, a longtime Trudeau friend, arranged a small party at her apartment on the Driveway in Ottawa to celebrate the fifteenth anniversary of Trudeau's prime ministership. It was a quiet affair attended mainly by political figures; Bill Kilbourn and I were the exceptions. Then, in September, Eleanor and I joined him and the Toronto Liberal elite at an official dinner for Prime Minister Margaret Thatcher in Toronto (nothing like the mob that had attended an intimate Ottawa reception for Vice-President Walter Mondale a few years earlier). The affair had its amusing moments including the seating plan that placed Dennis Thatcher beside Herb Gray. What had Herb done? I wondered. The centrepiece of the evening was an impromptu – though probably not first-night – debate between the two leaders. Both were skilled speakers who knew how to use logic, language, gesture, and tone of voice as weapons. Mrs Thatcher, in her most friendly fashion, made plain her opinion that Trudeau was a "wet." And he, in his most courteous manner, rebutted her every "neo-con" assertion. Both were amusing. As a debate, it struck me as a draw, though the new British Conservatism appalled me. But the assembled Liberals, I thought, displayed an ominous preference for the "Iron Lady." In John Turner's town, the natives were restless, yearning for tax cuts.

Governor General Ed Schreyer's dinner at the Chateau Laurier the following spring proved less entertaining. Diane Nelles, who was living in Ottawa at the time, went as my date. She reminded the prime minister that they had met several years earlier in Tokyo, and he seemed to remember. We sat with Eugene Whelan, his daughter, and Ed Schreyer's youngest son, Toban. I took to the minister of agriculture at once. So did Toban, who spent the early part of the evening sketching the man with the green cowboy hat. In return, Whelan teased him endlessly. Once his father began his farewell address, Toban dropped off to sleep, much to the envy of some of his dinner companions.

Trudeau devoted his final year in office attempting to promote nuclear disarmament and rapprochement between the two superpowers. Some viewed this frantic effort as a last attempt to win another election. Perhaps it was, though I had no doubt that, as so often, he meant exactly what he said. Peace and disarmament had deeply interested him since his pre-political days. His international activities as prime minister had often been a welcome respite from the constitution, inflation, and grain sales. Now, with the constitution out of the way, this last turn at promoting international peace and development was, in his judgment, natural. I joined with a number of others, led by Professors John Polanyi and Robert Laxer, to sponsor a full-page newspaper advertisement applauding his efforts. (I will always remember the pleasure of seeing Polanyi, a chemistry professor, correcting the grammar and syntax of a document composed by social scientists.) Some of the committee members decided to pay the prime minister a visit to encourage him further. I stayed home. His strenuous efforts failed, despite our support.

Neither gratitude for concluding the constitutional wrangles nor support for his peace mission appeared likely to give him and his party a new lease on power. Late on 28 February 1984 he took another long walk in the snow, with the predictable result. The following day he announced his intention of resigning. Unfortunately, before leaving office, he paid off an astonishing number of political debts with patronage appointments – a regrettably conventional way to end a remarkably unconventional career. Even his bad surprises were surprising.

As a fond farewell to my prime minister, I wrote a piece in the *Toronto Star* (see appendix 2) comparing him to Laurier, the same comparison he had implicitly asked me to make that night in January 1968 at the Royal York. (I did not mention that Laurier's patronage record exceeded his by many, many appointments!) Each of these prime ministers had succeeded intelligent but ineffective Liberal leaders and won electoral majorities. Each had come to power when relations between French and English Canadians had been in critical disarray. Each had found solutions to the cultural problems of their day only to see similar problems re-emerge later. This suggested that while Laurier's measures had worked for his times and Trudeau's had suited his, there could be no final solution in the search for accommodation between French and English in Canada. These continuing accommodations are the essence of our history.[1] Trudeau told me that he was pleased that I had remembered our conversation that night at the Royal York. It was only one of the most interesting of my life.

On rereading the piece later, I thought that I might have quoted Sir John Willison who, as editor first of the Liberal

Globe and then of the Conservative *News*, had been a fascinated lifelong Laurier watcher. "Laurier thought of Canada as a nation," Willison wrote in his *Reminiscences*. "He made Canada a nation, according to his panegyrists. Indeed with every change of government, Canada is made a nation over again. But the new pattern much resembles the old, however the artificers may labour to remould and rebuild."[2] Yet Trudeau had laboured to built a structure – the Canadian Charter of Rights and Freedoms – that ensured the future of his remoulding. Since my belief in the need for a constitutionally entrenched bill of rights had begun thirty years earlier when I was A.R.M. Lower's graduate student at Queen's, I was happy about the political choice I had made in 1968. That the Charter entrenched language rights, an item added to my original list in the 1960s, only increased my pleasure. In the first of his essays that I had translated in 1962, Trudeau had written of "Canadian federalism as an experiment of major proportions; it could become a brilliant prototype for the moulding of tomorrow's civilization."[3] Two decades later he had moved us in that direction. "He asked us to change," I told the convocation at York University in November 2000, "to grow, to govern ourselves in two languages, to respect human rights, and to celebrate all of our cultures." He had not "made us a nation over again," but he had lastingly remoulded the pattern by which a civic nation could flourish, a nation for patriots if not for nationalists.

DEFENDING HIS PATTERN

By 1984 Pierre Trudeau had spent nearly twenty years in the federal government's trenches. The first years of his retirement were quiet ones. Determined to avoid public attention and controversy, he settled into life in Montreal easily. His sabbatical (as he called it when people invited him to give speeches, accept honorary degrees, or sponsor causes) promised to be a private one. He could now take up his full responsibilities as the father of three fine sons, walk through the streets of Montreal to his law office (he went there regularly, he told me, so he could get some reading done free from crowds of tourists, some of whom sounded the doorbell at his impressive art deco house), ski, canoe, and attend book launchings. He joined old *Cité libre* friends at La Maison Egg Roll and more elegant venues. Occasionally he lent his name and his energy to prestigious international organizations that often were composed of other veterans of recent political wars. "For your information and possible action," he wrote on a copy of *A Universal Declaration of Human Responsibilities*, drawn up by the Interaction Council in 1997.[4] I signed on.

Occasionally when I visited Montreal we met for lunch, discovering a new shared taste for sushi. Once, after Eleanor and I had lunched with him and then parted, we later saw him striding down Sherbrooke Street on his way home from the office. I hailed him in order to introduce him to a visiting Japanese friend, Masako Iino, who was teaching at McGill. She was astonished that anyone would call a prime minister, even a retired one, by his first name. A few years later, when I debated constitutional matters at McGill, I asked if it would be all right to invite my son Mark (who was working at the National Film Board at the time) to join us at the Japanese restaurant. "Great idea," said Trudeau, "and I will bring Sasha." As usual, we bored our sons with our thoughts on the constitution while they looked on politely. Afterwards my sharp-eyed son asked if I had noticed that the green-labelled soya bottle had a sign on it reading "Mr. Trudeau's Soya." Of course I had missed that detail – evidence of blood-pressure problems. (In Japan, a personally labelled bottle would have contained much stronger drink!)

That we were discussing the constitution again in the late 1980s was thanks to Prime Minister Brian Mulroney, his friend Lucien Bouchard, Robert Bourassa and other provincial premiers, and assorted political scientists, chiefly from Queen's University. In the spring of 1987, responding to conditions set out by the Quebec Liberal Party for ratifying the 1982 constitution (and to attract Bouchard, whom Mulroney wanted as a cabinet minister in order to launder the record of scandal and incompetence established by his Quebec ministers since 1984), the prime minister had convened a First Ministers' Conference to reopen constitutional talks. The initial agreement, made public in early March, announced a completely new direction in constitution making. It recommended that a phrase should be added to the constitution designating Quebec as "a distinct society." What did that mean or imply? Was it a weasel phrase to describe a "special status" that flowed from an unstated premise that Quebec was the national state of francophones? When added to other proposals that weakened the Charter and the federal government's power in the area of social programs, this immediately struck me as threatening, especially since the federal government had given everything and gained nothing.

The day following the publication of the principles that would become the Meech Lake Accord, I broadcast a commentary on CBC radio entitled "What's the Cheering For?"[5] The title had first been used by John W. Dafoe, the great editor of the *Winnipeg Free Press*, in a denunciation of the Munich agreement on 30 September 1938. The pre-Meech principles, and later the accord itself, reversed the most important constitutional achievement of the Trudeau years. Quebec was now promised what nationalists had demanded unsuccessfully for decades, the first step towards establishing itself as a national state. This struck me as a tragic error, one confirmed in spades when the final accord appeared, making "distinct society" an interpretive clause to be applied to the entire constitution, including the Charter. The Bourassa government had originally requested that the "distinct society" phrase appear in the preamble, where it just might have been acceptable. It now appeared in the body of the constitution, associated with a provision that gave Quebec, and Quebec alone, the responsibility to "preserve and promote" this undefined "distinct society." Ian Scott, who was attorney general of Ontario at this time, later admitted to me that the "distinct society" clause had been "ratcheted up" because the other provinces rejected a constitutional veto for Quebec and demanded equality in the amending process. (In his wonderful autobiography, *To Make a Difference*, Scott revealed that his uneasiness about the ambiguity of "distinct society" had almost led to his resignation from the Peterson cabinet.)[6]

Having pronounced my preliminary assessment to a small, sleepy radio audience shortly after 8 AM, I mailed a copy to Trudeau, suggesting that he speak out. He probably didn't need my urging. Soon he appeared in full battle gear delivering polemics, as he liked to call them. His impact was enormous, much to the surprise and irritation of the first ministers and various others, some of whom naively believed that the accord would end Quebec's demands, and some of whom wanted to disfigure Trudeau's constitutional achievement.

The major mistake of the Mulroney government in 1987 was to reopen the constitutional question, which even in Quebec had lost much of its salience. Bourassa himself, according to

the journalist Andrew Cohen, had warned his new Conservative ally not to reopen it unless he was certain that it could be
settled.[7] Ever self-confident, and desperate for Bouchard's approval, Mulroney went ahead. The result was to provide the
divided and probably disintegrating Parti Québécois with an
energizing and reuniting cause. Almost immediately, its popularity began to revive and its march back to office began. Constitutional conflict was its lifeblood.

Prime Minister Mulroney's next mistake was to treat the accord as a done deal that needed little explanation or detailed
defence. The defence was left to his minister of intergovernmental affairs, Senator Lowell Murray, who had a reputation
as a deal maker, not as a constitutional expert. Effective defence would have required definition and clarity – the principal qualities that were lacking in the Meech Lake Accord.
Mulroney, Murray, and other supporters of the accord told
English Canadians that Meech Lake was largely a symbolic
response to Quebec's sense of rejection. Bourassa, and sometimes Murray when speaking in French, suggested that it was
something more – the beginning, not the end.

While Trudeau's influence in mobilizing public opposition
to the agreement was essential, the eventual collapse of the
Meech Lake Accord had much to do with the ineptness of its
supporters. First came Bourassa's use of the notwithstanding
clause to override a very moderate Supreme Court decision re-
specting the language of commercial signs. This action, he said,
would not have been necessary if Meech had been ratified. In
other words, Meech threatened English-language rights in Quebec. He then ostentatiously refused to support French-language
rights in a court case in Alberta, implying that each province
should deal as it pleased with its linguistic minorities. And finally, there was Prime Minister Mulroney's admission to his

admirer William Thorsell of the *Globe and Mail* that he had "rolled the dice." Since Trudeau had gambled and won in 1981, Mulroney may have thought he could do the same. All he got was the reputation of an irresponsible gambler – and he lost.

Here was the target on which, like Trudeau, I set my sights. Deborah Coyne, once my summer bank teller in Ottawa and in 1987 a lecturer at the University of Toronto Faculty of Law, called together a group whose aim was to promote critical public discussion of the Meech Lake Accord. I joined. It was, in fact, an opposition lobby. I also requested an opportunity to appear before the Special Joint Committee on the Constitution. My request was granted and my presentation made on 11 August 1987. I began with a detailed criticism of the accord, calling attention to the imprecision of its wording. Then I proposed amendments to clarify the relationship between the "Fundamental characteristics of Canada" and the "distinct society" of Quebec by giving predominance to the first. Finally, I urged that the accord be put to the people in either a general election or a referendum. It was a lively if fruitless discussion. Pauline Jewett, an NDP committee member, said my exchanges with the members reminded her of a good academic seminar; the newspapers called me "testy." When Lorne Nystrom said that my suggestion that all MPs should be working to extend French-language rights in their regions revealed my lack of knowledge of "the real world," I replied that my world was "real," his quite imaginary. Bob Kaplan, having ridden on Trudeau's coattails for fifteen years, had now taken up Meech, and tried to argue that French Canadians had voted against Confederation in 1867. I gave him the figures: twenty-seven for, twenty-two against. Afterwards we exchanged a few cool words about his right-wing deviation. When one Quebec Conservative accused me of wanting to perpetuate *cents ans d'in-justice*, I asked her for the list. I had never treated students in my seminars like that, but it was fun.

The *Canadian Parliamentary Review* asked permission to publish my submission. When the autumn volume appeared, "The Case for the Accord" was made by Premier Bourassa, "The Case against the Accord," by me. A photo of an animated Pierre Trudeau speaking to the Senate committee appeared at the end of my statement, perhaps for the benefit of the intellectually challenged – or perhaps it was guilt by association.[8]

Encouraged by Trudeau's entry into the fray, I prepared a more detailed explanation of my doubts about Meech. Robert Prichard, dean of the Faculty of Law at the University of Toronto, convened an academic conference for October to hear a variety of views on the Mulroney-Bourassa proposal. The more closely I analysed the accord, the more I concluded that its "fatal flaw" – something that Senator Murray had challenged his critics to discover – was the failure to define the central concept, "distinct society." I called my paper "The Concept of Quebec as a Distinct Society," later renaming it "Alice in Meachland" (at the time I did not realize that the Quebec topographical commission had changed Meach to Meech). My intention was to show that in Meechland, as in Wonderland, a name must mean something, as Humpty Dumpty had grumpily asserted. An undefined "distinct society" could lead only to claims and counter claims about its meaning and to permanent conflict, exactly the contrary of what its supporters promised. Ian Scott apparently agreed, for he later wrote: "Anything that rested on a fundamental ambiguity was doomed to failure at some point or other. Either the clause meant something or it meant nothing. If it meant something, then the other provinces would be upset when the courts explicated its content. If it meant nothing, then the deal would be forever criticized in Quebec."[9]

When Dean Prichard decided to open this academic symposium to a number of outsiders, including public servants and a few judges, I dropped out, publishing my paper later in the *Queen's Quarterly*.[10] This gave me the opportunity to use it as the basis for a presentation to a committee of the Ontario legislature established to consider Premier Peterson's pride and joy. There I heard my onetime student Charles Beer admit that the committee's work was window dressing, the real power being elsewhere. Then I crossed swords with Richard Allan of the NDP, a fellow historian, who tried to use me to put Pierre Trudeau in contradiction with himself. I declined, suggesting that Trudeau should be asked to speak for himself. I was getting to like these committee appearances.

Once drawn out of his self-imposed silence, Trudeau's performance was magnificent, bearing no relation to the uncivil, selective account presented by Gordon Robertson in *Memoirs of a Very Civil Servant*. That account never once dealt with the substance of the Meech Lake Accord, except by insinuating that opposition equalled denial that Quebec was "distinct." (In "Alice in Meachland" I had stated clearly that I had long taught that Quebec was "distinct" in a cultural sense.) Nor did it deal with Trudeau's critique. Still smarting under the thrashing he took from Trudeau in the *Globe and Mail* in October 1992,[11] Robertson was reduced to name-calling. His tactic was familiar enough. He tried it on me in a *Globe and Mail* exchange during the Meech Lake debate, revealing only his own inadequate reading of the accord's references to minority language rights; he inaccurately claimed that Meech guaranteed these rights. Robertson's willingness casually to dismiss the evidence provided by Bourassa himself that there was more to the accord than met a careless eye, displayed his naiveté about politics and a touching Mackenzie King–like belief that the highest political virtue is accommodation at any price.

While I did not much like anything in the accord, my initial goal was to obtain some changes. But the signatories, like the Fathers of Confederation with the Quebec Resolutions, adamantly refused to accept any amendments, at least until very late in the game. I could have reluctantly accepted inclusion of the phrase "distinct society" in the preamble to the constitution, provided it was merely descriptive. But what I could not accept was the application of this vague phrase in judicial interpretations of the Canadian Charter of Rights and Freedoms. Exempting the Charter from the "distinct society" clause became my minimum required change.

Here I found myself in total agreement with a determined group of lawyers – women lawyers who had fought hard and successfully to have equality rights included in the Charter. An ad hoc committee of LEAF (Women's Legal Education and Action Fund) was struck, funded by Nancy Ruth (Jackman), chaired by Marylou Macphedran, and including Mary Eberts and Anne Bayefsky. I was asked to participate. What a pleasure it was to work with organized, clear-headed people whose sympathies for their francophone colleagues and friends were as strong as mine! But like me they had decided that warm feelings and well-meaning promises were no substitute for clarity in constitutional language, an obvious lesson drawn from the history of constitutional disputes in Canada. We, mainly Mary Eberts, drew up a powerful case for modifying the accord in a fashion that would free the Charter from words whose vagueness invited unpredictable judicial interpretations. My experience with this thoughtful, high-spirited group of feminists reinforced my conviction that my untutored constitutional concerns were well founded.

Although Trudeau had entered the Meech debate with a bang, I heard nothing from him directly. Nor did I really expect to. I had asked him to speak out. He had done so, and I had thanked him. Then, in mid-November 1987, he wrote to say that he had been reading my critiques of the Meech Lake Accord and wanted to express his "support and admiration for the tireless attacks you have been launching against Meech Lake." He added: "I am convinced that the "distinct society" clause – if it is adopted – will set Canada irreversibly on the path towards some form of loose confederation, and from there into the lap of the U.S.A. So carry on the fight, like the little band at Thermopylae. But will we have our Salamis?"[12] Off to consult Thucydides again!

As early as 11 February 1988 he told me that he was beginning to think "that time may be on our side now."[13] At the end of a three-year battle, the little band had grown to a large throng, though its strength was never tested by an election or a referendum. The members of this motley coalition acted from a mixture of motives, not all of them generous by any means. The victory at Salamis, though never predictable, had been necessary. The Meech Lake Accord, and even more so its successor drawn up at Charlottetown a few years later, may have filled the prescriptions of political scientists and political opportunists; but those unhistorical remedies, ignoring – as both did – the concept of political nationality on which Canada was founded, offered no lasting cure to the country's ills.

This had been my conclusion after a debate at York with Professors Peter Hogg and Donald Smiley, both constitutional experts. Hogg admitted calmly that my critique was convincing, but judged it irrelevant. Important matters were often

left undefined, he said, and these were not even that important, since Quebec had not gained anything substantial. Smiley insisted that my earlier failure to demand definition for
every section of the Charter revealed my essential partisanship. He also contended, though he later admitted his error,
that the multicultural declaration in the Charter was no different from the distinct society clause. Another friendly opponent,
Professor Peter Russell, during a debate arranged for CBC correspondents at Niagara-on-the-Lake, suggested that my fears
were unjustified since the accord in fact changed little. Quebecers, being poor negotiators, had been satisfied with symbols.
Others seemed to act in the naive *bonne ententiste* belief that
something had to be done to satisfy Quebec, and Meech
seemed to be that something. This was the main line taken by
Senator Michael Meighen who, along with Senator Gérald
Beaudoin, jousted with Marylou Macphedran and me at a
Jewish senior citizen's home shortly before the end of the public debate.

These answers and others convinced me that Quebec would
eventually recognize the hollowness of the accord. Quebecers
– federalist and sovereignist alike – all expected words to mean
something. "If the recognition of Quebec as a distinct society
turns out not to mean anything," foxy Claude Morin wrote,
all the while licking his whiskers, "Quebeckers will begin
fighting again."[14] For Quebec sovereignists, the Meech Lake
Accord offered everything needed to jump-start their lagging
cause. If implemented, they could push it to its limits, an aid
to *étapisme*; and once those limits were reached, it could be
denounced as insufficient. If the rest of the country rejected
it, constitutional renewal could be proclaimed dead, leaving
only independence. Lucien Bouchard, the Bloc Québécois, and
the 1995 Quebec referendum rose from the ashes of the Meech

Lake Accord. So did Preston Manning and the Reform Party. The one thing Meech would never have achieved was what it promised – the appeasement of Quebec nationalism. In a radically and dangerously different context, this had been J.W. Dafoe's point in September 1938.

THINKING ABOUT THE RECENT PAST

April 1988 marked the twentieth anniversary of Pierre Trudeau's election as leader of the Liberal Party and his automatic move to the head of the cabinet table. A celebration was organized at the parliamentary restaurant, though the purpose of the gathering was not publicly announced. All the old Trudeauites assembled, black ties, designer dresses, and short hair having replaced the long hair, flared trousers, and miniskirts of 1968. Everyone looked older; even some of the "Pierrettes" had slightly matronly appearances. Jim Davey, who had died after a fall from his house while removing his storm windows, was missed. Eddie Rubin was lawyering in Hong Kong. Gordon Gibson, having long since traded his motorcycle for a place on the British Columbia right, looked uneasy. Tim Porteous and Marc Lalonde presided, administering an historical contest focused on 1968. The historian didn't win. Trudeau remembered everyone, it seemed, though nametags were supplied for greater certainty. There was some nostalgia, Liberals naturally preferring the good old days to a time dominated by Brian Mulroney. But mostly there was good-humoured recollection. Although no one said so out loud, the Trudeau years were over, and the time to treat them as history had arrived. That, at least, was what I thought the joyful celebration announced.

Once out of office, political leaders frequently begin to think about their record or, in the current journalistic cliché, their

For Ramsay
June 5. ?. 1988

The Trudeauites remember, twenty years after the first victory,
Ottawa, April 1988

"legacy." Political memoirs, autobiographies, and "official" biographies are intended to establish that record, to burnish that legacy. Trudeau was certainly interested in his record, but he was not particularly attracted by the idea of writing his memoirs. He hinted once or twice that he might like me to set the record straight for posterity, offering me access to his private papers. Since I had known him as a friend, it was not an unusual request, if that is what it was. He never asked directly or pressed me in any way. But I was certainly interested in his record.

Early in January 1989 he phoned to tell me that he and Tom Axworthy were planning a book of essays covering his years in office. He asked if I would contribute an essay to the book. I agreed. He next asked if I thought Marcel Trudel or Fernand Ouellet would be interested in writing something historical. I told him that Ouellet, whose interests were moving into the modern period, might do the job. And he did, writing a superb, heavily documented, greatly overlength socioeconomic analysis of the Quiet Revolution. (When the translator-editor demanded that he allow numerous extensive excisions and reductions of scholarly references or face rejection, I told her that if Ouellet was excluded, I would go with him. We both stayed.)

When invited to contribute to the book, I already had my essay ready. "I never thought I could be as proud ..." – The Trudeau-Lévesque Debate" – had originally been written for a Canadian Studies conference in London, England, in February 1988. The conference focused on these two leaders, heard from Richard Gwyn and me, and viewed *The Champions*, Donald Brittain's dramatic film about the Trudeau-Lévesque combat. Before I gave my talk, the head of the Quebec delegation in London politely introduced himself and said, laughingly, that he had come to make sure I would be fair to his leader, Premier Lévesque. At the end of the session he sought me out again, this time to congratulate me on my objectivity. I was surprised but satisfied. The agent general of Nova Scotia, a retired conservative politician who also attended the conference, was equally complimentary. Some months later, when I delivered a revised version of the paper as the Gray Lecture at the University of Toronto, I was criticized by a francophone member of the audience, who asserted that neither Trudeau's federalism nor Lévesque's independence was adequate; the correct answer to what Quebec wanted was "special status." Jelly never sticks to the wall.

The response to these two performances made me think that the lecture might be worth publishing. But one matter troubled me: I needed an exact reference to the statement that Trudeau had made following the 1980 referendum, and I asked him for it. After suggesting, not too subtly, that I might consult his archives, he said, "I can say with certainty that I meant the sentence to be an exact parallel to Lévesque's."[15] That, of course, had been the point I had made at the end of the essay, for the remarks dramatized my comparison of these two political leaders. Trudeau's response made me think that I should ask him to read the essay, hoping he might offer me some other helpful details, or that he might join the Quebec delegate in complimenting me on my fairness to Lévesque. So I sent it off, commenting that if the current election ended in a minority, "the little band of Thermopylaens may still reach Salamis!"[16]

His reply came quickly: "Let us only hope that more of us survive than did in Leonidas' day." Then he turned to my paper. Of course, he picked out the usual typing errors and

French misspellings; he was a demanding proofreader. Then he wrote a paragraph that was both generous and characteristically perceptive about our friendship: "Your essays, I always rejoice in reading, and this one was no exception. I enter into your thought processes as one enters into a room and suddenly experiences 'déjà vu.' Or more exactly, something akin to saying: 'He sees things exactly as they happened, or at least as I saw them happen …' – which I hope is not demeaning of your objectivity as an historian."[17] This last remark caught me utterly by surprise, not because the thought had never occurred to me, for it certainly had, but because it had occurred to him.

Over the years since 1968, I had often thought about the relationship between the historian and the prime minister. In the early years of our friendship, we had discovered that we shared ideas on a certain number of important subjects, nationalism, federalism, and civil liberties being the most important. After 1968 Trudeau embodied these ideas and possessed the power to advance them, or, as I realized in October 1970, to depart reluctantly from them. How did that power affect our relationship? Since I continued to share and support his essential ideas, had I now become merely an apologist for him? What about my supposed objectivity as an historian, the question he was now raising?

Insofar as I ever resolved this problem, I did it along these lines. First, when historians comment on contemporary affairs, their arguments are often informed by historical knowledge. That does not make their comments "history"; they remain contemporary comment, a form of journalism. Second, I had never hidden my commitment to certain ideas, and that doubtless coloured my historical writing as it did my contemporary comment. I had been taught and believe that historical objectivity is both desirable and unobtainable, not because historians are dishonest but because historians are humans – what Peter Novick meant when he described the quest for scientific objectivity in history as *That Noble Dream*.[18] Often, though perhaps not always, I attempted to be detached, or at least analytical, in my contemporary comment. Even when writing about Trudeau, the historian who once was his speechwriter tried to explain the politician's ideas and decisions rather than simply defending them. The line between explanation and justification can, of course, be a fine one.

Then there is the question of power. Was explaining, even defending, ideas attached to power more compromising than explaining or defending ideas free from that corrupting influence? My answer was negative. I had always found it easier to defend relatively powerless minority ideas than I did defending the only prime minister I had ever voted for. In the final analysis, I knew that in writing about my friend Pierre Trudeau's ideas I was writing contemporary comment, not history. In doing so, I expressed, I hope frankly, my own intellectual preferences. On matters of nationalism and federalism, I had no doubt that I saw things very much the way Trudeau did. Those were convictions I had held long before he entered politics – indeed, even before we had become friends. Even so, I believed that writing about René Lévesque's sovereignist option in a fair, explanatory fashion was not beyond my range or responsibility as a trained historian and committed contemporary commentator. My essay on Trudeau and Lévesque demonstrated, I think, both my training and my commitment.

I certainly did not find Trudeau's comments on my essay "demeaning of [my] objectivity as an historian." That the idea actually occurred to him, and that he told me so, revealed again the person whose intellect and generosity I had long since learned to admire. I never once felt that our intellectual or personal friendship required me to sacrifice my objectivity as an historian or that it compromised that supposed objectivity. Others were probably less convinced.

Towards a Just Society was a curiously mixed book, neither autobiography nor history. It included historical essays, as well as thoughtful reflections by the former Trudeau cabinet ministers Marc Lalonde and Gérard Pelletier, public servants Tommy Shoyama and Ian Stewart, and political aides Tom Axworthy and Jim Coutts. Trudeau contributed a systematic outline of "The Values of the Just Society," a document essential to an evaluation of his liberalism. The reviews of the book were fairly negative. Dale Thomson, a McGill political scientist who had written sympathetic studies of two Liberal prime ministers and one Quebec Liberal premier, charged both Fernand Ouellet and me with corrupting ourselves as historians by appearing in this politically engaged book. Exactly what sin we had committed that he had avoided, he failed to explain. Perhaps he could not.

The sales of *Towards a Just Society*, like all Trudeau books, soared. The proceeds, after consultation among at least some of the contributors, were used to revive *Cité libre* in the summer of 1991, just as Quebec nationalism, reignited by the Meech Lake debate and defeat, was again threatening Canadian federalism. Trudeau was very pleased at the magazine's revival. He had often complained that the nationalists, as in Duplessis's time, had gained a near monopoly over public discussion in Quebec, while federalist voices had fallen almost silent. Quebec, we all believed, needed a liberal, antinationalist voice again. Anne-Marie Bourdouxhe, Gérard Pelletier's daughter, assumed the thankless task of editor and carried out her responsibilities superbly for the next four years. I contributed an article on *Le Devoir* to her last issue in the summer of 1995. It was like old times, though Trudeau fired his broadsides at the Charlottetown Accord from La Maison Egg Roll. He had not returned to writing for his old magazine (and never did).

THESE TENTATIVE MEMOIRS

In my conversations with Trudeau about *Towards a Just Society,* I regularly urged him to settle down to writing something more extensive about his life, at least his public life.[19] At first he showed some interest and asked if I would help him, or write a book of my own. I was willing to do what I could in whatever time I had, because I thought he had a wonderful book in him if only he could be persuaded to apply himself to writing it. By offering to help and perhaps to write a book about his years in office, I hoped to spur him on. But nothing happened, though his pen remained sharp, as various exchanges over the constitution in the press demonstrated.

In March 1989 I wrote him a long letter filled with unasked-for advice about memoirs. I told him that there were two options, the first being several volumes of heavily documented "official" history, written on the basis of research reports prepared for him or even drafts of chapters that he could touch up. Lester Pearson's memoirs had been done this way. Such tomes were valuable, though they would never be accepted as definitive and might be as boring as Paul Martin's lengthy ruminations. Obviously, I was not urging him to take this choice. Then, thinking that a little ego-stroking might move him to write the sort of book that I believed he could do brilliantly, I continued (typos again corrected):

The second alternative is something more personal. Pelletier has captured this very well – except that he has modestly chosen to leave himself out! An older version of this were [sic] the memoirs of Chubby Power (I can't find my copy at the moment but I remember that a political scientist named Norman Ward helped with the writing of this wonderful volume). Though not political Claude Lévi-Strauss's *Tristes Tropiques* or even John Stuart Mill's *Autobiography* is what I have in mind. You reflecting on your life and work (sorry to sound pompous). You write so well, especially when you are in a slightly (!) engaged mood. So you should write a book explaining how you arrived at the views you held in the 50s and 60s, why that led to a political career as a Liberal, and why what you tried to do in power to test your ideas against the demands of Canada. You could choose the themes you wanted, comment on the people and events that seem appropriate, write reflectively but without any pretense to so-called "scientific" history."

As if this was not inflated enough, I went further:

Now you might say: people will respond to this type of book by saying, oh it's just Trudeau's *Apologia pro vita sua* or his *Confessions*. My response is to say: exactly, that is what it is and for that reason it will last just as the Augustine and Newman and Rousseau and Levi-Strauss's books lasted. That is, in a way, [what] René Lévesque tried to do; he failed because he was in too much of a hurry, too anxious to get in some cheap shots against his enemies and, of course, he never was a reader or a writer, so he had no understanding of the genre. (The same might be said of Jean Chrétien's enormously popular memoir – amusing to read but without much lasting value.)[20]

Again I offered to help, but the offer was never taken up. We discussed it further during a visit that Eleanor and I had with him in Montreal. But flattery got me nowhere. He told me he couldn't write either kind of book, he couldn't get interested enough to spend the time. His style, he said, was the polemical article not reflection on the past. Not yet ready to give up, I tried again, sending him articles by Václav Havel and Adam Michnik. (He replied that he especially admired Havel's *Power of the Powerless*, my favourite too.) But his mind was still on the present, on Canada and Quebec. It was August, after Meech had blown away, when he wrote:

Who would have predicted that Meech would collapse thanks to the combined efforts of the first and of the last Canadians? In Quebec, there prevails a kind of peaceful satisfaction that our bonds with Canada have been slackened: an ominous situation in a country which is leaderless. And political depravity has reached the state where the government party and the NDP could run avowed separatists in a by-election without provoking more than a few tut, tuts!

In such times, maybe Eleanor's poetry [in fact, our daughter Margaret's poetry] and my memoirs are of secondary importance. There is such a falsification of history afoot, that the *real* historians will have to roll in like thunder on the left.

But, as the Portuguese say: "The worst is not always certain."[21]

During these months of discussion, Trudeau had told me that he was being pressed by the CBC to cooperate in the production of a television series on his years in office similar to the series that Cam Graham had done on Diefenbaker and Pearson. Graham had tried to enlist me in the project, doubtless at least partly because he knew that my involvement might reassure a reluctant Trudeau. I was certain that Graham would produce an excellent documentary on the Trudeau years and looked forward to playing some role in it. I had worked with him on several occasions years earlier, appearing in his *Tenth Decade* series and once, during the 1974 general election, flying with him in a private plane to Trois-Pistoles to interview Réal Caouette at his chosen place and time – after *Hockey Night in Canada*. (Robert Mackenzie of the London School of Economics interviewed the other leaders in less interesting places at less watched times.)

Trudeau's handlers, I subsequently heard, played tough, wanting more control over the final editing than Graham would accept, and no deal was struck. Instead, guided by his friend Gérard Pelletier, he agreed to participate in a TV memoir produced by Brian and Terrence McKenna, two excellent, controversial filmmakers. Once the agreement was reached, Trudeau told me he hoped that I would participate in some part of the series once the producers had a script outline. I agreed, thinking that I would appear as someone who had known him for quite a long time and had worked with him in the 1968 election. So instead of discussing my role in the McKennas' plans, I simply accepted a request to take part when Kevin Tierney first approached me about the series. It soon transpired that I would be cast as a "Liberal historian," twinned with Michael Bliss, a "Conservative historian," to discuss the Trudeau government's record. I withdrew. Trudeau friend and supporter, yes; but Liberal historian, *nyet*. The man from central casting reported Trudeau's disappointment at the news; but, typically, Trudeau made no attempt to change my decision. Michael Bliss appeared alone and did a good job as a contemporary commentator.

The TV series drew a huge audience and received lukewarm to harsh reviews from the critics. I enjoyed it, though like most programs of that sort it didn't dig very deep. Not as deep, I suspected, as Cam Graham would have gone. The subject and the series' success made it inevitable that a print version would follow. One day in the summer of 1993, Doug Gibson of McClelland and Stewart called me at Tenpenny Lake to ask if I would be willing to read the manuscript of Pierre Trudeau's memoirs. He told me that the book was essentially a reshaped version of the TV series. Naturally I agreed, curious what the end result of all my failed efforts would look like. I read it, found a few errors and omissions (I was especially surprised at the absence of any mention of gender equality rights in the Charter), and with a sense of resignation concluded that, poor thing that it was, it was all we would get.

I first read Trudeau's preface after *Memoirs* appeared. There he spoke of the book's origins, of his serious reservations about autobiography, going over all the points we had discussed, even referring directly to some of the arguments I had pressed on him. I was a little relieved, but not surprised, to read that he "was unwilling to appoint an official Boswell" to whom he "would feed a self-serving version of events." He was almost apologetic – not a characteristic public stance. He had taken the "easy" way, and the result was, he said "a personal and in-formal account of my political life as I remembered it when prompted by questions from the interviewers."[22] Good grief!

Trudeau's *Memoirs*, of course, was an enormous success. The launchings and abbreviated book tour re-created the Tru-deaumaniacal scenes of 1968, dismaying him as much as it did then. I skipped the Toronto launch but attended the sumptu-ous dinner that Avie Bennett hosted at the Grand Yatt Dynasty Restaurant. As the evening commenced, Larry Zolf burst in to say hello, reminding me that in his bizarre book *The Dance of the Dialectic*,[23] back in 1973, he had actually displayed some understanding of my support of Trudeau's ideas. Trudeau greeted him in a warm fashion while others scowled at this voluble interloper. Later in November I attended the launch at the National Archives, where my old friend Jean-Pierre Wallot (once a PQ riding association president and now national archivist) made his first ever complimentary speech about Pierre Trudeau. Again the crowds gathered around in the polite way expected of invited guests. A reporter asked me how I thought Trudeau compared to other Canadian prime ministers. "He is *sui generis*," I mumbled evasively. "Would you mind spelling that?" he replied. When I recounted this to Pierre, he said something about the continuing need to enforce the Official Languages Act in Ottawa.

For several months I waited for Pierre to send me a copy of his book. After all, I had used up a few sunny days at the cottage reading the manuscript (McClelland and Stewart didn't send me one either). When it didn't come, I reminded him that he owed it to me.[24] Soon it arrived, still in the bookstore bag. I supposed he had either dropped into Smith's on the way home or sent someone out to buy it – no author's free copy or even author's discount. In it he had written, "For Ramsay Cook, these tentative *Memoirs*, with apologies to the historian and a thousand thanks to the loyal friend." As always, he knew where we stood.

KEEPING UP THE FIGHT

Despite his declared permanent sabbatical, Trudeau could still be provoked into discussion, both private and public, about the constitution and the state of the world. Having won the battle of Meech, he next weighed in against the Charlottetown Accord, once again aiding its opponents. One performance that invited comparison with a much younger Trudeau was his convocation speech at the opening of the Bora Laskin Law Library at the University of Toronto in March 1991. Trudeau usually refused to accept honorary degrees, but his admiration of Bora Laskin, whom he had appointed chief justice over a more senior judge, convinced him that he should participate in this ceremony. But he was not prepared merely to utter the usual convocation platitudes. Instead, with retired Justice Brian Dickson sitting in the front row and the presence of numerous other legal luminaries, he chose to defend Laskin's dissenting opinion in the *Patriation Reference* of 1981. It was both closely argued and cheeky.[25]

A full house at Simcoe Hall sat listening to a man who could make constitutional law seem important. The judicial leaders squirmed, and Dickson's neck grew red. Afterwards, Professor Peter Russell felt compelled to set the former prime minister straight in the university *Bulletin*. Others, especially very civil servants, took the view that the old man had simply been rude. But what did they expect? Asked to speak to an academic audience on an occasion honouring the memory of one of the country's finest legal minds, what could have been better than a defence of Laskin's dissent from the fuzzy majority decision on patriation? Those who were embarrassed knew neither Pierre Trudeau nor Bora Laskin, himself a forthright intellectual.

There was a dinner that night at President Prichard's house for the rich and famous, and doubtless for judges and legal scholars. There must have been a few tense moments and some highly diplomatic ones. Trudeau had asked me to gather a few of his Toronto friends for breakfast at the presidential mansion the following morning. Albert and Margot Breton, Fernand

and Thérèse Ouellet, and Eleanor and I joined Rob Prichard and his wife for a delicious unbreakfastlike repast and invigorating conversation. Trudeau was in good form. We teased him about his *lèse majesté* the previous afternoon. "Ask a serious man to a serious occasion, and he makes a serious speech," he said, his eyes twinkling. He had obviously enjoyed his performance. The host said little, perhaps fearing that his formidable guest might ask him to account for his presence in David Peterson's tent in the last days of Meech Lake. (Not long afterwards I had an unseemly, *au naturel* shouting match with the former premier in the Glendon College locker room, when Peterson denounced Trudeau and then me for our attacks on Meech. That day I swam more than my customary mile.) At Prichard's breakfast party, Trudeau was warm and gracious, as always, making sure the wives present were not left out of the conversation. So there was poetry as well as politics.

During the next few years Trudeau came to Toronto occasionally, visiting his daughter Sarah and her mother Deborah Coyne. Sometimes he would call or we would get together with mutual friends. One Saturday afternoon, after he had enjoyed a long outing with his daughter, a group gathered at Deborah's for the usual constitutional discussion. He claimed that he was not really up to date with what was going on any more, but he proved no slouch with the scholars and journalists present. I especially remember how attentively he listened to Professor Lorraine Weinrib's defence of the notwithstanding clause as a strength rather than weakness of the 1982 constitution. It forced the premiers to defend their positions publicly and made the Charter a model for countries like Israel and South Africa, she argued. It was a hard sell, for Trudeau believed that the notwithstanding clause was a high price to have paid – and he had paid it – to get nine premiers to sign on in 1981. But he was partly convinced. "I'll accept your arguments as a second line of defence," he told her. This was a substantial concession.

Professor Weinrib's assessment of Trudeau's constitutional achievements, published in the Montreal *Gazette* after his death, was wise and just. Its title would have pleased him immensely: "A Liberal Democracy by Design." She wrote: "Trudeau's legacy includes not only legal substance but political process as well. The process by which the 1982 amendments became part of the supreme law of Canada also gave us a singular experience in political leadership. The popularity of the Charter that paved the way for its adoption, the continuing widespread support for the Supreme Court's constitutional judgments, and the repeated resistance to invocation of the notwithstanding clause all stand as his legacy."[26] Trudeau's 1968 promise of "participatory democracy" had been fulfilled, at least temporarily, during the years of constitutional conflict between 1980 and 1992.

TOWARDS THE END

We talked a couple of times when I visited Montreal, usually over Japanese food. Mostly it was politics and the constitution but the conversation always covered personal things – our children and his, or his recent painful ear operation to remove a bone spur so that he could continue scuba diving. Eleanor sent him a poem by Richard Wilbur called "To His Skeleton," which described the development of bone spurs in the poet's ears ("Why will you vex me with / These bone-spurs in the ear?"), and Trudeau reported his pleasure in discovering that such pain could be turned to poetry. On one of these occasions he told me of his search for a Canadian history book to translate into Spanish for Mexican readers, and I suggested the one that Craig Brown had put together, *The Illustrated History of Canada*. He took up the suggestion and got it done. Occasionally he seemed to hint that I might still write something. After a dinner with him that John Fraser of Massey College arranged in January 1997, I suggested that I might publish a study of the role that his government and its policies had played in defending French Canadians and promoting French Canadian culture in Canada.[27] He replied that he had promised to cooperate with Ron Graham on a book of excerpts from his writings and speeches, and he thought that would be enough Trudeau for now. *The Essential Trudeau* reduced his thought to the sayings of Chairman Pierre. Since I was about to take up a second visiting professorship for a term at Yale, I was just as glad that he had not encouraged my proposal. Yale seemed a good opportunity, once again, to free my mind of Canadian controversies.

From Yale I sent Trudeau a copy of a very critical review I had written of Ken McRobert's *Misconceiving Canada,* an attack on Trudeau's constitutional policies. McRoberts and I had taught a course on Quebec together for several years after I first arrived at York. A good scholar with an extensive knowledge of contemporary Quebec, he believed that "special status" was what Quebec deserved and what would satisfy its national ambitions. Dualism, Quebec and English Canada, required constitutional recognition. I disagreed. That made for good teaching, since students needed to debate various viewpoints. But his book struck me as naïve about nationalism and politics, and animated by a personal dislike of Trudeau. My review said so. I sent it to Pierre, remarking that he "needed to be kept straight on these matters." He replied, "Your quip about me needing 'to be kept straight on these matters' is not unwarranted: in arguing in favour of institutional bilingualism, it is possible that I might sometimes have sounded like a dualist!

But certainly not in a constitutional sense."[28] This display of word play greatly reassured me, for I had begun to hear rumours that he was no longer his old self. Yet here he was, spirited as ever, and announcing a trip to Japan and China. Surely his health was sound.

The first sign that I was right to worry came in January 1998 when the English edition of *Cité libre* was launched in Toronto. Max and Monique Nemni had taken over the editorship, and would soon turn it into a defender of pure Trudeauism. Although I did not realize it at the time, their assumption of control had left quite a few wounded in its path. Trudeau agreed to attend the Toronto event. He was the drawing card; several of his old opponents, somewhat sheepishly passing through the hastily assembled receiving line, were obviously pleased to shake his hand. But he refused to speak in public. So others, including Jean-Louis Roux, the great man of the Quebec theatre, and I, filled in. I presented a brief history of the magazine. Trudeau sat in the front row, so I teased him a little, saying that Eleanor and I had once translated his "lousy French," a phrase he had used to describe his fellow Quebecers' language many years earlier. He laughed. I ended with an unidentified quotation, which he obviously recognized as his own: "Les hommes ne peuvent vivre libre et en paix que si leur société est juste."[29] I hoped that would please him, too, since it demonstrated that his quest for a "just society" had been announced in the 1950s.

During the early part of the evening, I noticed that he fended off questions; he told the journalists that he couldn't remember much about the early days of *Cité libre*. I thought it was just his usual ploy, though I had heard that this proud man was worrying about short-term memory difficulties. (I knew that he went on memorizing poetry to combat memory loss.)

Pierre Trudeau with admirers at the Toronto launch of the
English-language *Cité libre*, January 1998

Afterwards we went together to dinner. At the Metropolitan
Hotel, he seemed briefly confused, though everything seemed
fine when we sat down to a splendid feast of Chinese food. He
obviously wanted his friends near: Jacques Hébert, Jean-Louis
Roux, Eleanor and me. When I suggested that we let other guests
take our place, he said he wanted to be with his friends. He
seemed fine, though uncharacteristically anxious about the time
of his flight departure. When I arranged for a young woman from
the Donner Foundation, who had written a thesis on Trudeau's

ideas, to go with him to the airport, he seemed enormously relieved. I thought he had overexerted himself, just a normal sign of advancing age.

Looking back now, and with the photograph that Des Glynn of Ryerson University took of him that night as he looked on while I lectured him, I see a man growing old faster than I realized at the time. The skin is pulled more tightly than ever on his sculptured face, and there is a look in his eye that is not the Pierre of 1968, or even of 1997. I did not see this picture until Glynn left it for me a few days after Pierre's death. The photo revealed a warning I had not wanted to recognize.

"WHO HAS SEEN THE WIND"

Over the next year we talked a few times on the phone, mainly about personal matters. Once he wondered if my son Mark could help his son Sasha find some assistance with a film he was editing. But I never saw him again. When Misha died in an avalanche, his father's face at the funeral showed a broken man. Who could break Pierre Trudeau? his critics had wondered. Now the answer was obvious: the death of a beloved son, the one who had pressed clawing crayfish on us at Harrington Lake in the summer. "He is the mischievous one," Pierre had said. His letters now became a sentence or two: "What a beautiful birthday gift you have given me: *Krieghoff/Images du Canada!* I am looking forward to many pleasant hours of reading and looking."[30] Signed, as usual, "In friendship."

A visit was obviously the obligation of a friend. But I put it off. I did not want to face what I now knew I would see for myself. Then it was too late. When I phoned in mid-July 2000, his secretary said he was spending most of the summer with his boys. We agreed that, as usual, he had made a good decision.

He would be in the office again in mid-August, she said. I should call again. He did not return. When I called on 25 September, I was told that Mr Trudeau was seeing no one.

Rumours about Trudeau's failing health had been circulating for months, though as usual he had tried to protect his privacy. Late in June, minutes after arriving at our cottage at Tenpenny Lake, a reporter from *Maclean's* called on an obituary mission. The ghoulish rush had begun. I had nothing to say; Pierre Trudeau was still alive. Soon the first crisis passed. Another frenzy began in mid-September, but I had decided to be silent. Mourning friends should mourn. Death came on 28 September. When the news finally arrived – my son Mark heard it first and phoned – it left me numb. The next day, as the numbness subsided, grief and depression took its place.

Then came the question: What is to be done to mark this friend's departure? Go to Montreal for the funeral? Go to Ottawa to the casket lying in state? Do nothing? The last seemed both best and impossible. Montreal seemed too public, too many people being seen. Not being there had its advantages. Driving to Ottawa to join the lines of "ordinary Canadians," as the CBC called us, would mean going to the place where I had often met Pierre. So Eleanor and I went on the spur of the moment, just after Saturday's usual shopping trip to the St Lawrence Market. On Sunday morning, with our daughter Maggi, we joined the throng waiting to enter the Centre Block. I glanced over at the second-floor window of the East Block, where I had spent so much time in the spring of 1968. Ottawa had been the right choice – the crowds a respectful, sober re-creation of the excited ones that had swarmed around Pierre in 1968. "I have come to bid farewell to my brother," a woman who had emigrated from the Caribbean just after Trudeau became prime minister told a television reporter. After thirty-two years, his magnetism, even in death, had not dissipated.

Passing his official portrait in the foyer (more benign than pensive, it fails to catch the power of Pierre's gaze) brought back all the memories. The flag-draped coffin brought a crisis. Soon it was over. Then we were out in the sunshine where the mourners and the curious multiplied. I gathered two red Parliament Hill maple leaves, imitating a French-speaking family. Tenpenny Lake for lunch. There, at last, in the autumn sunshine, with the leaves nearing their autumnal brilliance, the depression lifted. Maggi and I removed the rigging from the sailboat. I thought of the name that we had given it: the "W.O. Mitchell" of *Who Has Seen the Wind*, now so appropriate. Driving back to Toronto on Sunday afternoon, I knew we had made the right choice. The sorrow had become manageable. The indelible memories of a friendship remained.

If you, that have grown old, were the first dead,
Neither catalpa-tree nor scented lime
Should hear my living feet, nor would I tread
Where we wrought that shall break the teeth of Time.
                                        W.B. Yeats[31]

APPENDICES

What's Special about the NDP's Status for Quebec?
The Globe and Mail, 3 August 1967

There was a time when Pierre Trudeau, the Minister of Justice, was viewed by liberally minded persons in English and French Canada as a brilliant and lucid thinker and writer. But that has passed. Mr. Trudeau has become a politician.

Today, he is a favourite target of French-Canadian nationalists and English Canadians who identify themselves with the New Democratic Party. Quebec Premier Daniel Johnson, Ontario NDP Leader Donald MacDonald, and many of Mr. Trudeau's old friends in the NDP denounce him for his failure to accept the latest cliché of Canadian constitutional discussion: a special status for Quebec.

States his mind
The trouble with Mr. Trudeau, as a politician, is that he states his mind frankly. That used to be a quality admired in the NDP, but in recent years its leaders have fallen more and more into the old Liberal formula for calculated ambiguity. There is no better example than the phrase special status. In the constitutional debate, Mr. Trudeau has put

his position with his usual clarity on a number of occasions. He believes, in effect, that if the federal government treats Quebec as a distinct nation within Canada, Quebec will ultimately become a distinct nation outside of Canada. Special status, no matter how limited, would be the first step, to be followed by others, making Quebec more and more special until it became independent.

Consequently, Mr. Trudeau favors a federalism that provides equal status for French Canadians and equal status for all provinces. He believes that this can be achieved within the framework of the existing constitution, by insuring that the jurisdictions of federal and provincial governments are observed, and by the implementation of practical measure of bilingualism.

Mr. Trudeau's reasoning is much more subtle than his critics have allowed. It is based on carefully considered conclusions about Quebec, modern nationalism, and the demands of a technological age. These ideas are expressed in his writings for the past 15 years, most of which appear to have been ignored by experts in "Trudeauism." The view is brilliantly summed up in a lengthy, still unpublished memorandum which he prepared for presentation to the Quebec Legislative Assembly's Committee on the Constitution. (The nearest approach to Mr. Trudeau's views is found in the brief presented to that same committee by the Quebec Federation of Labor, the Confederation of National Trade Unions, and the Catholic Farmers' Union – a brief which nowhere advocates the concept of special status.)

Two propositions

Mr. Trudeau's views are perhaps summarized in two propositions. The first: "It is always costly and inefficient to choose men and favor institutions on the basis of their ethnic origin rather than according to criteria of aptitude and competence." The second proposition follows from the first: "I am opposed to what it is convenient to call a special status for two reasons, among others: I would not do Quebeckers the injury of pretending that their province, in order to progress inside of Confederation, has need of favored treatment: moreover, I believe that in the long run that can only tend to weaken the values which we ought to submit to the proof of competition. Even more than technology, a culture progresses only by exchanges and challenges; and, in Canadian federalism, French cultural values can find a happy mixture of competition and protection from a state that is strong enough."

Mr. Trudeau may, of course, be wrong. So honest and perceptive a man as Claude Ryan of Le Devoir thinks so. In Mr. Ryan's view, Quebec must have a special status if the forces leading to complete separation are to be appeased. But even Mr. Ryan apparently sees special status as a mere stopping point on the way to some further expression of autonomy for Quebec. (This is a view held by several significant Quebec nationalists – Father Richard Arès, for example – who see special status as a step in the gradual evolution of Quebec toward full nationhood.)

Writing in Le Devoir on June 30, Mr. Ryan said: "We believe that it is possible and desirable, at least for one or two generations, to maintain a federal regime in Canada, on the condition, however, that this regime consecrates in law and in fact a distinct position of Quebec under the form of a special status." In short, Mr. Ryan's analysis really confirms Mr. Trudeau's contentions – a fact almost totally ignored by English-speaking proponents of special status.

The real difficulty is that little serious consideration has been given to this question in English-speaking Canada. This was evident at the recent convention of the New Democratic Party in Toronto. Almost no one, with the exception of a few members of the policy committee, showed any sign of understanding the nature of the special-status proposal. That, at least, is the most charitable explanation. The floor debate was brief and almost wholly irrelevant. Robert Strachan, British Columbia NDP leader, got the debate off the rails with emotional remarks about the excess of Chinese over French in British Columbia. Laurier LaPierre proved that he could answer irrelevancy with irrelevancy. The resolution passed in a euphoric atmosphere, with the delegates convinced that the French-Canadian problem has been solved again.

Around the corner

Power must surely be just around the corner: with a resolution in favor of special status and the federal caucus, or at least one member, on record as favoring the recognition of St-Jean-Baptiste Day as a national holiday, how could French Canadians continue to resist the NDP?

In the discussion of the constitution at the convention, by far the most interesting statement was made by the Quebec leader, Robert Cliche. This French-Canadian John Diefenbaker delighted his audience with a lengthy denunciation of Mr. Trudeau. The burden of his denunciation, accompanied by head-shaking and arm-waving, was that Mr. Trudeau, supported by the "namby-pamby" Liberals from Quebec, is guilty of misleading English Canada in his insistence that Quebec will accept the constitutional status quo. (He didn't produce any concrete evidence to prove that Mr. Trudeau actually does support the status quo.)

Parallel charge

Mr. Cliche's charge was especially interesting, since it is parallel to another charge brought against Mr. Trudeau by some unofficial spokesmen for the NDP. Harry Crowe and Douglas Fisher, in their syndicated column, have repeatedly insisted that Mr. Trudeau is guilty of misleading French Canada by his insistence that English Canada accepts his decentralizing views on the constitution. English Canadians are, in reality, centralizers, Messrs. Crowe and Fisher insist (ignoring Premiers W.A.C. Bennett, John Robarts, Duff Roblin, and even Robert Stanfield, as well as a certain amount of Canadian history), and they want more and more of their affairs handled in Ottawa. The syndicated journalists are clever in their use of language for they summarize Mr. Trudeau's position thus: "What is good for Quebec is good for the rest of us." The spectre of "Quebec domination" immediately leaps from the heated English-Canadian imagination. And who is to save us? At least we can be thankful that it is not the New Democratic Party with its magic formula, a special status for Quebec.

But what does the formula mean? Reading through the speeches of NDP Leader T.C. Douglas; Andrew Brewin, member of Parliament for Greenwood; Mr. MacDonald and Mr. Cliche, nothing strikes one more forcibly than the vagueness of every reference to special status. Speaking in the Ontario Legislature on May 18, Mr. MacDonald repeated his frequently stated view that Quebec should have a recognized special status in Confederation. He then went on, not to explain the content to this status, but rather to suggest that perhaps Mr. Robarts' Confederation of Tomorrow Conference could define this status. But since special status is Mr. MacDonald's declared policy, it might just be reasonable to expect him to define its content.

A few days earlier in Ottawa, Mr. Douglas and Mr. Brewin had not been much more helpful. Mr. Douglas moved an amendment in the Throne Speech debate condemning the Government for its failure to grant Quebec a special status and then proceeded, as The Globe and Mail remarked, to "discuss everything else on earth except this special status, which he neglected to mention again." It was probably just as well, because his infrequent statements on constitutional matters (including those at his press conference after his keynote address at the NDP convention) indicate a shaky grasp of the problem. Consequently he usually leaves constitutional matters to Mr. Brewin.

Mr. Brewin, speaking in the House on May 15, grappled manfully with the problem of special status. In the middle of his speech he uttered the following revealing sentences: "If I understand the doctrine propounded by the Minister of Justice, it is that the present constitutional arrangement, interpreted in such a way that the federal Government should stay strictly out of the fields of provincial jurisdiction, is quite sufficient to satisfy the aspirations of the Province of Quebec. I do not know whether this is so. However it may be, there is no reason why this doctrine should be accepted by the rest of Canada. There may well be fields of action in which federal intervention is desired by the other provinces although unacceptable to Quebec. If so, the device of a special status for Quebec can be used to meet the aspirations of Quebec on one hand and the rest of Canada on the other. I am afraid I have no time to give illustrations showing how this would apply."

Playing word games

Since the remainder of Mr. Brewin's speech covers almost three full columns of Hansard, one is left wondering if his inability to illustrate the theory was entirely a problem of time. Still, his statement is an important one, for it makes plain the fact that the NDP is playing word games, and deceptive ones at that.

What the NDP's concept of special status boils down to, surprisingly, is not a special status for Quebec, but rather a special status for the English-Canadian provinces. In the NDP view, Quebec will be allowed to exercise fully the powers granted to it by the present constitution. At no time has any official NDP spokesman suggested that Quebec should be granted any of the powers held, exclusively or jointly, by the federal Government. In short, the NDP accepts, for Quebec alone, the Trudeau position that the federal constitution should be strictly observed. But the other provinces will not have the same privileges.

Opting-out rights

Accepting what is very close to the French-Canadian nationalist position expounded by Professor Michel Brunet of Montreal – that Quebec is the national government of Quebeckers, Ottawa is the national government of English Canada – the NDP insists that when Quebec opts out of federal programs the other provinces should not be allowed to do so. No other interpretation can be placed on repeated criticisms which NDP spokesmen have made of the current Liberal view that when Quebec opts out of a federal program, all other provinces must have an equal right.

Thus the special status which the NDP advocates is nothing other than special status conferred upon the provinces of English Canada by the progressive diminution of their powers through federal initiatives. All that will be special about Quebec is that it will continue to live under the existing division of powers. In reality, then, the NDP has not done any new thinking on the constitution. Instead, it has attempted a mixed marriage between the centrist concepts of the Rowell-Sirois Report of 1940 and the decentralist concepts of Quebec's Tremblay Commission of 1956. It is extremely doubtful that the marriage will bear the bountiful electoral fruit that the NDP obviously anticipates.

The reasons are simple. In the first place, nobody, not even the most moderate proponents of special status in Quebec (Mr. Ryan, for example) look upon the present powers granted Quebec under the constitution as satisfactory. Mr. Ryan has made this point repeatedly, even in his speech to the NDP convention. On that occasion he applauded the NDP for adopting the special-status idea, but called upon the party to define its content.

The fact is that the NDP has accepted a general formula which will arouse an emotional appeal in some Quebec circles. However, it has refused to give the formula any substance, because there is no agreement on the meaning of the term that would be acceptable to English-Canadian NDP members which would not strip the slogan of its propaganda value in Quebec. But the irony of this situation is that Mr. Cliche, who vigorously denounced Mr. Trudeau for defending the constitutional status quo, is himself committed to a view of special status which would not increase Quebec's constitutional powers in any significant fashion. Either that or Mr. Cliche and his Quebec supporters are not saying the same things about special status as Messrs. Douglas, Brewin, and MacDonald.

Second problem

The second problem is just as serious. From a tactical point of view there is not much reason to think that the idea, how-

ever, vague, of a special status for Quebec is an attractive
one in English Canada. And when it is explained that the
special status is not really for Quebec at all, but rather for
the other provinces, the effect will likely not be very noticeable. For the reality is that the English-Canadian provinces
do not have the propensity to abdicate their powers that the
NDP doctrine assumes they do. It was not Quebec, but rather
Ontario, Alberta and British Columbia who scuttled the
Rowell-Sirois Report in 1940. None of these governments in
the past 25 years has been observed pressing Ottawa to take
over provincial powers. And no one who has paid the slightest attention to the briefs presented by Ontario to federal-
provincial conferences in the past six years can doubt the
views of the Robarts Government. There is very little reason
to think that this position would be changed, even if, by
some near-miracle, the NDP took power in Ottawa and in
each of the provincial capitals. On that millennial day, Mr.
MacDonald would begin to sound like former Ontario
Premier Mitchell Hepburn, Robert Strachan like former B.C.
Premier Duff Pattullo, and Neil Reimer like former Alberta
Premier William Aberhart when speaking of provincial jurisdictions. The weakness of the NDP lies in the superficiality
of its analysis of Canadian federalism, a weakness which it
inherited from its predecessor, the CCF. The CCF did not
really accept federalism, which it believed, in Harold Laski's
phrase, had been made obsolete by capitalism. In the years
of the Depression this view made some sense, though the
Canadian electorate never accepted it. The NDP at its founding convention in 1961 seemed ready to put the Nineteen
Thirties behind it and embrace a new federalist view of
Canada. Since then the trend has been back to the old position. It is ironic that it was none other than Mr. Trudeau

who, in Social Purpose for Canada published in 1961 to give the NDP some intellectual foundations, warned the party against just this possibility. "Unfortunately, Socialists in Canada," he wrote, "have seldom been guided in their doctrine and their strategy by a whole-hearted acceptance of the basic political fact of federalism."

Difficult country?

The latest NDP proclamation on Canadian federalism indicates that the party still sees federalism as something to circumvent, rather than one of the prime necessities of Canadian existence. Canada is a difficult country to govern, it has often been remarked. The NDP appears to believe that it is a difficult country to govern because it has a federal system. The truth, and it is a truth which Mr. Trudeau has recognized, is that Canada has a federal system because it is a difficult country to govern.

Ramsay Cook

History Will Measure Trudeau against Laurier
Ramsay Cook, Special to the *Star*, 4 March 1984

When Pierre Trudeau was pondering the question of running for the Liberal party's leadership in the spring of 1968 he asked a friend: "If I become prime minister, will French Canadian historians treat me the same way that they have treated Laurier?"

The question was very revealing. First of all it meant that Trudeau saw that former prime minister Sir Wilfrid Laurier was the past leader against whom he had to measure himself – and would be measured.

That was natural enough for a French Canadian and a Liberal. But it also revealed, again not surprisingly, that Trudeau was aware that though Laurier remained a hero for the general public in Quebec, the white-maned knight had not received such a good press in the Quebec history texts.

For Quebec nationalists, and nearly every historian in Quebec is a nationalist, Laurier's legacy was an ambiguous one. While he was the first French Canadian to become prime minister, the Canada he presided over during a 15-year period (1896–1911) had caused French Canadians some anxieties.

Hardly rosy

Laurier himself had claimed that just as the 19th century had belonged to the United States, so the 20th century would belong to Canada. But from the French Canadian nationalist viewpoint the view was hardly that rosy.

Laurier, from the nationalist viewpoint, was denounced as a man more interested in staying in office than in defending the rights of French-speaking Canadians. He was a great compromiser which meant, the nationalists claimed, that he conceded too much to the English Canadian majority.

Had he not, despite initial opposition, sent Canadian troops to the Boer War? Had he not, despite a half-hearted attempt to give legal protection to the minorities in the West, finally sold out in the face of concerted English Canadian pressure? Had he not, while claiming to favor the construction of a Canadian navy, slipped into the Naval Bill a clause which would allow that navy to be transferred to the British fleet in time of crisis?

Always the compromiser – "waffley Wilfie," Henri Bourassa called him.

And for nationalists like Bourassa, who founded Le Devoir in 1910 to fight Laurier, there was no doubt that Laurier was much more under the influence of his English Canadian colleagues than he was willing to admit.

Was national unity, the goal to which Laurier devoted his life, merely a rhetorical cloak used to hide the fact that French Canadian rights were being sacrificed on every side?

In the end fate was to save Laurier from the final condemnation of his nationalist compatriots. Electoral defeat in 1911 left Laurier out of office during the Great War when relations between French and English Canadians almost reached the breaking point.